A2

STUDENT'S BOOK

BEYOND

MACMILLAN

Robert Campbell
Rob Metcalf
Rebecca Robb Benne

Grammar (2): *This/that/these/those,* plurals, object pronouns

Vocabulary (2): Classroom things, colours, the alphabet

PRONOUNCE the /iː/ sound

LISTENING & VOCABULARY	GRAMMAR (2)	LANGUAGE & BEYOND	SPEAKING	WRITING
Meet my family **Listen for the main ideas** **Vocabulary (2):** Family	*Have got* **Talk about relationships and possessions**	Communicate & cooperate: **Understand different ways to say 'hello'**	How do I get there? **Ask for and give directions** ▶ Go straight on	Hello from St Petersburg (e-postcard) **Use correct punctuation**
Let me show you round **Use sounds to help you understand** **Vocabulary (2):** Furniture and other things in the home	Present simple with adverbs of frequency **Talk about how often you do things**	Get organised: **Organise your things**	When's the next one? **Ask for and tell the time when you travel** ▶ What time's the fast train?	My favourite room (description) **Use also and too**
Dress code **Listen for specific information** **Vocabulary (2):** Clothes and accessories PRONOUNCE The /əʊ/ sound	Possessive *'s, whose* and possessive pronouns **Talk about possessions and relationships**	Know yourself: **Understand your learning style**	What are they like? **Describe people** ▶ She's got brown eyes	Things we do and like (A questionnaire) **Use and, or and but**
Soundscape **Identify the type of audio** **Vocabulary (2):** Places in public buildings	Present continuous and present simple **Talk about how often you do things**	Get thinking: **Find ideas and information**	At the tourist information office **Ask for information** ▶ Can I ask a question?	School concert (A notice) **Use headings**
Food for the brain **Identify the speaker** **Vocabulary (2):** Lifestyle adjectives	*Like + -ing* **Talk about your likes and dislikes**	Respect others: **Follow the rules in electronic communications**	I don't believe it! **React to news** ▶ Wow!	My favourite meal (description) **Use because**

LISTENING & VOCABULARY	GRAMMAR (2)	LANGUAGE & BEYOND	SPEAKING	WRITING
Game over **Understand spoken instructions** **Vocabulary (2):** Games verbs **PRONOUNCE** The /uː/ sound	*Have to* and *don't have to* **Talk about things that are and aren't necessary**	Communicate & cooperate: **Work with others in a team**	*Can I?* **Ask for and give or refuse permission** ▶ Is it OK if I go?	My sporting hero (profile) **Use paragraphs**
Dear Diary **Use pictures to help you listen** **Vocabulary (2):** Personality adjectives	Past simple positive **Talk about completed events in the past** **PRONOUNCE** Past simple *-ed* endings	Get thinking: **Understand what makes people creative**	Guess what? **Tell an interesting or funny story** ▶ It was really funny	My diary (blog post) **Use time expressions**
The amazing story of Palle Huld **Take notes** **Vocabulary (2):** Forms of transport **PRONOUNCE** Stress on important words in sentences	Past simple questions and short answers **Ask and answer questions about the past**	Get organised: **Plan for a night away**	Check in and out of a hotel **Ask for repetition** ▶ We have a reservation	A message from Mexico (email) **Use descriptive language**
Radio ads **Use important words to help you listen** **Vocabulary (2):** Money and measurements	Superlative adjectives **Compare one thing with the others in a group** **PRONOUNCE** The /ɜː/ sound	Respect others: **Listen actively to other people**	What would you like? **Buy things at a market** ▶ I'd like …	The best place in town! (advert) **Check your writing**
World days **Identify positive and negative feelings** **Vocabulary (2):** Feelings	*Will* for predictions **Predict things in the future**	Know yourself: **See things in a positive way**	Congratulations! **Give wishes and congratulate people** ▶ Good luck!	Let's celebrate! (invitation) **Use typical phrases in invitations**

IRREGULAR VERBS page 140   **EXTRAS** pages 141–142   **PROJECTS** page 143

GET READY: ENGLISH 24/7

3

WELCOME to THE ENGLISH SUMMER CAMP
DRAMA SPORT MUSIC
ALL IN ENGLISH 24/7

SUMMER CAMP

Hi. My name's Marta.

2

July

M	T	W	T	F	Sat/Sun
1	2	3	4	5	6 / 7
8	9	10	11	12	13 / 14
15	16	17	18	19	20 / 21
22	23	24	25	26	27 / 28
29	30	31			

Today's Monday, the fifteenth of July. It's the first day of Marta's summer camp.

THINK AND READ

1 **Work in pairs. What can you do at a summer camp? Write three more activities.**

   meet new friends _____
   eat different food _____
   speak in English _____

2 ▶1.01 **Read the story. Which things in Exercise 1 does Marta do on her first day at summer camp? Why is today a special day for Marta?**

3 **Read the story again. Do the exercises when you see this icon** ⭐.

RECALL

1 ⭐ **DATES**

   a ▶1.02 **Write the dates from the calendar. Listen and check. Then listen and repeat.**

   15/07 = It's Monday the fifteenth of July.
1 03/07	3 20/07	5 21/07
2 12/07	4 25/07	6 02/07

   b **Write the names of the other months. Then write and say today's date.**

2 ⭐ **INTRODUCTIONS**
Complete the introductions with words from the table.

I	you	he	she	we	they
my	your	his	her	our	their

1 Hi. *We* 're Japanese. _____ names are Kaori and Shiro.
2 This is Sergei and _____ brother, Pavel. _____ 're Russian.
3 Hello. I'm Turkish. _____ name's Alara.
4 This is Silvia. _____ 's Spanish. Her sister's here too.

3 ⭐ **NATIONALITIES**

▶1.03 **Write the nationalities. Listen and check. Then listen and repeat.**

Country	Nationality
Mexico	*Mexican*
Germany	
Italy	
Japan	
Russia	
Spain	
Turkey	

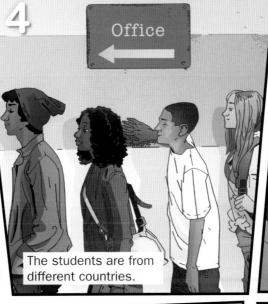

4

Office

The students are from different countries.

5

Hello. My name's Marta.

Hi Marta. I'm Cesco. Where are you from?

I'm from Italy. My dad's Italian but my mum's German.

I'm from Mexico City. I'm Mexican.

6

What's your name?

It's Marta.

7

When's your birthday?

It's today.

Thank you.

Really? Happy birthday, Marta!

8

And what's your name?

---

4   ⭐ **BE**

▶1.04 **Complete the conversation. Then listen and check.**

Max: What (1) _'s_ your name?
Marta: It (2) _____ Marta. Marta Esteban.
Max: There's another student called Esteban. (3) _____ you brother and sister?
Marta: No, we (4) _____ . He (5) _____ my brother.
Max: Where (6) _____ you from?
Marta: I (7) _____ from Mexico. I'm Mexican.
Max: How old (8) _____ you?
Marta: I (9) _____ 14.
Max: When (10) _____ your birthday?
Marta: It's today.

5   ⭐ **PERSONAL INFORMATION**

a   **You're one of the students in the picture. Think of a new name and nationality. Then complete the form for 'You'.**

	You	Your partner
Name		
Surname		
Nationality		
Age		
Birthday		

b   **Work in pairs. Complete the form with your partner's new information. Ask questions from Exercise 4.**

What's … ?   *How old … ?*

Where … ?   *When's … ?*

c   **Introduce your partner to other students.**

This is …

He/She's from …

He/She's … years old.

This is your classroom.

THINK AND READ

1 Complete the things you usually do at school.

r e _a_ d	w r __ t __
l __ s t __ n	s p __ __ __ k
r __ p __ __ t	c h __ c k

2 (►1.05) Read the story. Tick (✓) the things you see from Exercise 1.

3 Read the story again. Do the exercises when you see this icon ⭐.

RECALL

1 ⭐ **CLASSROOM THINGS**
(►1.06) Write the letter (a–l) of the things in the classroom in the picture. Listen and check. Then listen and repeat.

_a_	board		floor
	chair		light
	clock		poster
	computer		table
	desk		wall
	door		window

2 ⭐ **COLOURS**

a (►1.07) Write the colours. Listen and check. Then listen and repeat.

b Work in pairs. Talk about the colours in your classroom.

My pen's blue.   *Yes, and the …*

3 ⭐ **THE ALPHABET**

a (►1.08) Listen and write the missing letters in the correct place. Then listen and repeat.

A	B	C̶	Đ	E	F	G	H	I̶	J	K	L	M̶
N	Ɵ	P	Q̶	R	S	T̶	U	V	W̶	X	Y	Z̶

/eɪ/	/iː/	/e/	/aɪ/	/əʊ/	/uː/	/ɑː/
A	B	F	I	O	Q	R
	C					
J	D	M			W	
	G	S				
	T	Z				

b (►1.09) **PRONOUNCE** Listen and repeat the words with the /iː/ sound.

he	she	r**ea**d	sp**ea**k	rep**ea**t	gr**ee**n
th**e**se	m**e**				

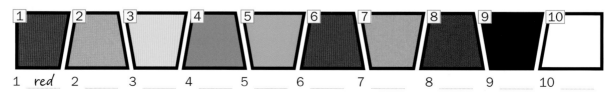

1 _red_	2	3	4	5	6	7	8	9	10

4 ⭐ THIS, THAT, THESE, THOSE

a **Complete the table.**

	here ↓	there →
Singular		
Plural		*those*

b **Work in pairs. Ask the name of things in the classroom. How do you spell the names?**

What's that?   *It's a …*   *What are these?*   *They're …*

How do you spell it?

5 ⭐ PLURALS

a ▶1.10 **Listen and write the words.**

b **Write the plurals of the words.**

6 a ⭐ OBJECT PRONOUNS

▶1.11 **Complete the conversation with the object pronouns in the box. Then listen and check.**

her	it	~~me~~	them	us	you

Marta: Can you help (1) _____ *me* _____ ?
Cesco: Sure.
Marta: Where's my pen? I can't see (2) _____ .
Cesco: It's on your desk in front of (3) _____ .
Marta: Right! And the teacher? I can't see (4) _____ .
Cesco: There. She's looking at (5) _____ because we're talking. Where are your glasses?
Marta: I don't know. I can't find (6) _____ .

b **Where are Marta's glasses?**

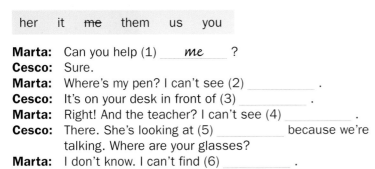

7 ⭐ Work in pairs. Which things in Exercise 5 can you see in the classroom picture?

Where's / Where are … ?

It's/They're here/there.

8 ⭐ SAY GOODBYE
Say goodbye to your teacher and other students when your class finishes.

UNIT 1 WELCOME TO MY WORLD

IN THE PICTURE In town

>>> Talk about places in a town

WORK WITH WORDS Places in a town

1 a **RECALL** Work in pairs. Put the words in the correct order from big (*1*) to small (*6*). You have one minute.

____ town	____ street	____ flat/house
1 city	____ town centre / city centre	____ building

b Complete the words for the places. You have two minutes.

1 You watch plays here. t_____
2 You swim here. s_____ p_____
3 You play sports here. s_____ c_____
4 You see animals here. z_____
5 You buy things here. s_____
6 You eat meals here. r_____
7 You watch films here. c_____
8 You walk and play games here. p_____

2 Look at the map and the photos. What city is this?

3 a ▶1.12 Listen to Teresa. Put the places in the photos in the order you hear them (1–10). What other place does Teresa talk about?

b ▶1.13 Listen and check your answers. Listen and repeat.

4 a ▶1.14 **PRONOUNCE** Listen to the places in the box. Choose the correct word for the explanation. Listen again and repeat.

> airport castle library station tower

> When a word has two syllables (sounds), the stress is usually on the *first* / *second* syllable.

b Say these words with the correct stress.

> building centre city concert cricket football

5 ▶1.15 Choose the correct words to complete the conversation. Then listen and check.

Sienna: Hi Teresa. Where are you going?
Teresa: To the (1) *square* / *library* to get some books. Then to the (2) *airport* / *station* to meet my grandma from the train. She wants to go to the art (3) *castle* / *museum*.
Sienna: Is she here for a few days?
Teresa: Yes. Tomorrow she wants to do shopping at the (4) *theme park* / *shopping centre*. And at the weekend she wants to see the cricket match at the (5) *tower* / *stadium*. She loves cricket!

WELCOME TO MY CITY!

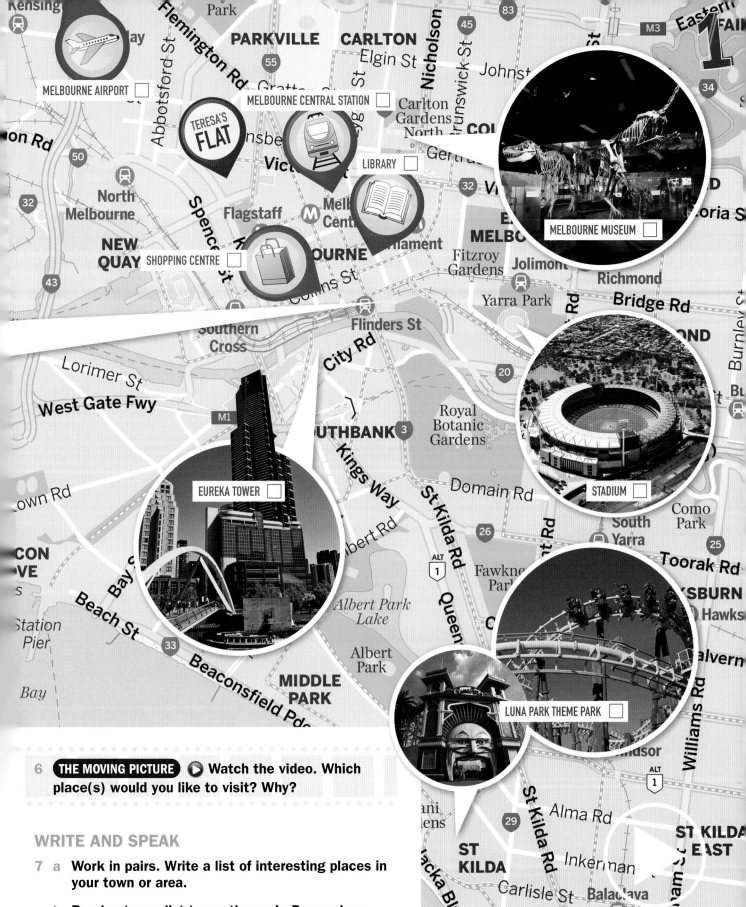

MELBOURNE AIRPORT ☐

TERESA'S FLAT

MELBOURNE CENTRAL STATION ☐

LIBRARY ☐

SHOPPING CENTRE ☐

MELBOURNE MUSEUM ☐

EUREKA TOWER ☐

STADIUM ☐

LUNA PARK THEME PARK ☐

6 **THE MOVING PICTURE** ▶ Watch the video. Which place(s) would you like to visit? Why?

WRITE AND SPEAK

7 a Work in pairs. Write a list of interesting places in your town or area.

b Read out your list to another pair. Do you have the same places? What are your favourite places?

> *On our list we've got the technology museum, …*
>
> *My favourite place is …
> (because …)*
>
> *We've got the technology museum too.*

GO BEYOND ⏩

Do the Words & Beyond exercise on page 130.

>>> Identify the type of text

SPEAK AND READ

1 **Work in pairs. Look at the title of the page. Together, choose the correct explanation for 'sister cities'.**

A cities in the same area with the same number of people
B cities in different countries with a special link
C cities in different countries with the same language

2 a **Read the tips in the** HOW TO **box.**

b ▶1.16 **Use the tips in Exercise 2a and try and identify the type of text. Then read the text and check.**

A a magazine article
B a 'What's on?' website with a list of events
C an online city guide
D a guidebook

HOW TO ❓
identify the type of text

☐ Read the titles.

☐ Look at the text. Does it look like a train timetable, an article, … ?

☐ Look at the photos and the pictures.

CITY GUIDE

| Things To Do ▼ | Shopping ▼ | Art & Culture ▼ | Food & Drink ▼

OUR SISTER CITY *Osaka*

Melbourne **Extra**

Extra tips, extra information, extra fun!
Melbourne has six 'sister cities':

■ Osaka, Japan (our first sister city in 1978)
■ Tianjin, China (1980)
■ Thessaloniki, Greece (1984)
■ Boston, USA (1985)
■ St Petersburg, Russia (1989)
■ Milan, Italy (2004)
Follow the links and find out more.

Two and a half million people live in Osaka. The city has two main centres: Namba and Umeda. In Namba at the famous Bunraku Theatre you can see plays with one-metre-high Japanese puppets. There are also many good shops and cinemas.
Near the station in Umeda, there's a big shopping centre under the city. The HEP Five shopping centre is also there and it's got a hundred-metre-tall big wheel on the roof! There are also lots of cafés and restaurants – people in Osaka love food.
Osaka Castle is very popular with visitors. In the main tower there's a museum about the castle's long history. Visit the castle in the spring and have a picnic in the beautiful park next to it.

3 **Which tips in the** HOW TO **box did you use for help with Exercise 2b? Tick (✓) them.**

4 **Teresa is making notes on Melbourne's sister cities. Read the text again and complete her notes. Use one word, number or date.**

Number of Melbourne's sister cities:	(1) _six_	
Osaka: sister city from:	(2) _____	
Number of people in Osaka:	(3) _____	million
Bunraku Theatre:	(4) one-metre-high	
Umeda shopping centre:	(5) _____	the city
Big wheel:	(6) _____	metres high
Osaka Castle:	(7) _____	in the main tower

REACT

5 🗨 **Work in pairs. What do you think? Tell your partner, giving reasons for your answers.**

1 Would you like to go to Osaka? Why?/Why not?
2 Has your town or city got sister cities? Where are they?
3 Why are sister cities a good idea?

PHRASE BYTES 📱

… sounds interesting/boring …
My town's sister cities are …
You can learn about …

GO BEYOND ⏩

Write the nationalities for the countries in the text.

>>> **Describe what's in a place**

READ >>> Grammar in context

1 **Read the chat messages. Where does Owen live? How many people live there?**

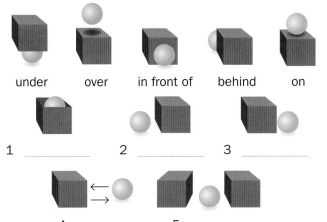

> **ANTONIO:** Where do you live?
>
> **OWEN: In** New York.
>
> **ANTONIO:** Wow! Are there any towers **next to** your home?
>
> **OWEN:** No, but there are some small houses.
>
> **ANTONIO:** Is there a sports stadium **near** you?
>
> **OWEN:** No, there isn't. And there aren't any parks.
>
> **ANTONIO:** Is there a zoo?
>
> **OWEN:** There isn't a zoo but there's a farm **opposite** our house.
>
> **ANTONIO:** Oh. Are there any shops?
>
> **OWEN:** Yes, there are. … Well, there's one shop **between** my grandma's house and our house. There are only 15 people here.
>
> **ANTONIO:** But you live in New York City!
>
> **OWEN:** No, I live in New York, Texas! :)

STUDY

2 **Complete the explanations. Use Exercise 1 to help you.**

There is / there are

Use: To describe what's in a place.

Form:

Positive
There's a … / There _____ (some) …

Negative
There _____ a … / There aren't (any) …

Questions and short answers
Is there a … ? / Are there any … ?
Yes, there is. / _____ . No, there _____ / aren't.

See GRAMMAR DATABASE, page 120.

3 **Look at the pictures. Complete 1–5 with the correct words in bold from Exercise 1.**

under   over   in front of   behind   on

1 _____ 2 _____ 3 _____

4 _____ 5 _____

PRACTISE

4 **Write sentences about New York City.**

1 some tall buildings ✓
   There are some tall buildings.
2 a big park ✓ _____
3 big farms ✗ _____
4 a lot of people ✓ _____
5 a beach ✗ _____
6 a lot of quiet places ✗

5 **Complete the sentences about the picture. Use *there is / there are* and prepositions of place.**

1 _There are_ some shops _in_ the square.
2 _____ a restaurant _____ one of the shops.
3 _____ some trees _____ the museum.
4 _____ a bookshop _____ the museum.
5 _____ some tables _____ the café.
6 And _____ me _____ the chair!

SPEAK AND WRITE

6 **Student A: Look at the picture on page 141. Student B: Look at the picture on page 142.**

▪ Describe your picture to your partner.
▪ Draw your partner's picture. Then compare it with the picture in the book.

7 **a** **Write the questions for a survey.**

> **Is your town or area a good or bad place for young people? *We want to know!***
> ① there / a theme park / in your area?
> ② there / a sports centre / near your home?
> ③ there / any parks?
> ④ there / a swimming pool?
> ⑤ there / free concerts in your town?
> ⑥ there / other places for young people?

> **b** **Write your answers. Tell the class if your town or area is a good place for young people.**

>>> Listen for the main ideas

SPEAK AND LISTEN

1 RECALL **Work in pairs. Circle 12 family words.**

MOTHER QUIET DAD BIG LONELY SISTER CHILD
MUM LIVE LIKE BORING HOME FATHER
NOISY ASION GRANDFATHER GRANDMA
BROTHER HAPPY SMALL
GRANDCHILD
GRANDAD GRANDMOTHER

2 a **Read the tips in the HOW TO box.**

b ▶1.17 **Listen to four students in the pictures. Have they got a big family or a small family?**

3 ▶1.17 **Listen again. Circle T (true) or F (false).**

1	Riley thinks a small family is nice.	T/F
2	Akari's family watches a lot of TV.	T/F
3	Akari thinks it's noisy at home.	T/F
4	In Antonio's flat it's always quiet.	T/F
5	Jessie's mum isn't married to Jessie's dad.	T/F
6	Jessie is sometimes lonely.	T/F

REACT

4 **Work in pairs. Answer the questions.**

1 What's good about a small family?
2 What's good about a big family?

WORK WITH WORDS Family

5 ▶1.18 **Work in pairs. Complete the sentences with the correct words. Listen and check your answers. Then listen and repeat.**

Riley lives with his sister and his (1) _____ . He's their (2) _____ . His sister is their (3) _____ . (daughter / parents / son)

Akari's (4) _____ s live with her family. She's their (5) _____ . Her four brothers are their (6) _____ s. (grandson / granddaughter / grandparent)

Antonio's mum has three brothers – Antonio's (7) _____ s. She also has two sisters – Antonio's (8) _____ s. They have lots of children – Antonio's (9) _____ s. (aunt / cousin / uncle)

Jessie's mum is (10) _____ to a new (11) _____ . Jessie's dad has a new (12) _____ . (married / wife / husband)

6 **Work in pairs. Write the names of five people in your family. Show your partner the names and answer questions.**

Who's Nisha?

She's my aunt. She's married to my Uncle Oliver.

HOW TO

listen for the main ideas

- Don't try to understand every word.
- Listen for words you know.
- Use these words to help you understand important ideas.

GET TO KNOW

STUDENTS FROM MELBOURNE AND ITS SISTER CITIES!

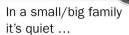 WHAT'S ON STUDENTS SEARCH

Talking point: *big and small families*

PHRASE BYTES

In a small/big family it's quiet …

It isn't lonely/boring/ noisy …

Riley, MELBOURNE

Akari, OSAKA

Antonio, MILAN

Jessie, BOSTON

GO BEYOND

Do the Words & Beyond exercises on page 130.

GRAMMAR *Have got*

>>> **Talk about relationships and possessions**

READ AND LISTEN >>> Grammar in context

1 **1.19 Read and listen to the conversation. Who's Josh?**

Lucy: Have you got any brothers or sisters?
Riley: Yes, I have. I've got one sister.
Lucy: Have you got any pets?
Riley: No, I haven't. But my sister's got a cat. It's got long black hair and it hasn't got a name. We call it 'Cat'. What pets have you got?
Lucy: We haven't got any pets. But I've got a little brother. My parents call him Josh but I call him 'Noisy'.

STUDY

2 **Complete the explanations with examples from Exercise 1.**

Have got

Use: To talk about relationships and possessions.
I've got a sister.
My sister's got a cat.
It's got long black hair.

Form:

Positive
I/you/we/they've got
he/she/it _____ got

Negative
I/you/we/they _____ got
he/she/it hasn't got

Questions and short answers
_____ I/you/we/they got … ?
Has he/she/it got … ?
Yes, I have. / No, he hasn't.

See **GRAMMAR DATABASE**, page 120.

3 **Start a chain sentence in your class. One student starts. Then the next student repeats and adds another thing.**

I've got a brother.
I've got a brother and a dog.
I've got a brother and a dog and a …

PRACTISE

4 a **Complete the description with the correct form of *have got*.**

My favourite cousin

I (1) *'ve got* _____ lots of cousins but my favourite cousin is Viktor. He (2) _____ black hair. I don't see him much because he doesn't live near us and his parents (3) _____ a car. But they (4) _____ a computer and we often chat online. He (5) _____ the same interests as me; we like different things. But we (6) _____ always _____ lots of things to talk about.

b **Write three or four sentences to describe one of your family members.**

c **Work in pairs. Read your sentences to your partner.**

5 a **Write the questions for other students in your class. Use *have got*.**

1 you / got / a big or a small family?
Have you got a big or a small family?
2 how many cousins / you / got?
3 you / got / any pets?
4 your family / got / a house or a flat?
5 what colour hair / your mum / got?
6 your parents / got / a car?

b **Write one more question. Use your own ideas.**

SPEAK

6 a **Stand up and walk round the class.**
- Ask other students the questions in Exercise 5.
- Find two students with the same answer to each question. Write the students' names.

b **Tell your partner.**

Talaz and Deniz have got a big family.

Carmel and Franco haven't got any pets.

Hugo's mum and Tam's mum have got black hair.

LANGUAGE & BEYOND

'Hello Mrs Matthews. How are you?'

'Hi Keesha.'

'Good morning!'

'Hey Jerome! How's it going?'

'Hello, nice to meet you.'

>>> Understand different ways to say 'hello'

SPEAK AND READ

1 **How many different people do you say hello to on a school day?**

  ▪ Make a list of their names and the places. Compare with a partner.

2 **Look at the pictures of Marie's morning. Does Marie know the other person? Is the other person a friend?**

DO

3 **Read these tips. Are they the same for your country?**

4 **Match the tips (a–g) to pictures (1–5) above.**

a	Use first names for friends and family.
b	Use *Mr/Mrs* or *Ms* plus surname when you don't know adults well.
c	When you meet somebody for the first time, say 'Nice to meet you.'.
d	Use a formal greeting with strangers, older people, teachers, etc: 'Good morning / Hello'.
e	Use 'Good morning' before 12pm, 'Good afternoon' after 12pm and 'Good evening' after 6pm.
f	Use an informal greeting with friends: 'Hi' or 'Hey'.
g	Ask about somebody's health: 'How are you?' (formal), 'How's it going?' (informal).

a _2, 4_

School eXchange tips

In the UK ...
» look the other person in the eye.
» smile.
» only hug or kiss good friends or family.

REFLECT

5 🗨 **Talk about the questions. Then read the** **REFLECTION POINT**.

  1 When do you say hello to strangers in your country?
  2 What are informal and formal greetings in your country?
  3 Why do you think it's important to use people's names?

PHRASE BYTES

We always say hello to strangers in shops …

A formal/informal greeting is …

It's important because people feel …

EXTEND

6 a **Work in pairs. Act out the situations in Exercise 2. Add replies.**

  b **From today, say hello to your teacher and classmates in English.**

REFLECTION POINT

It's important to say hello to people in the right way. Be friendly but show respect. Use people's names, so they feel special.

Workbook, page 17

COMMUNICATE & COOPERATE

⟩⟩⟩ Ask for and give directions

SPEAK

1 Work in pairs. In a new place, do you ...

– ask for directions?
– use a map?
– use your phone to find the way?
– often get lost?

WATCH OR LISTEN

2 ▶️▶️1.20 Watch or listen to the scenes. Why can't the last person give directions?

1
Alex: Excuse me, can you tell me the way to the shopping centre?
Rose: Yes. Go straight on for 200 metres. It's on the left.
Alex: Thank you.
2
Amy: How do I get to the library, please?
Luca: Turn left. Then take the second right. It's next to the museum.
Amy: Thanks.
3
Joe: Can you tell me the way to the station, please?
Skye: It's just round the corner. You can't miss it.
Joe: Thanks.
4
May: Excuse me, I think I'm lost. How do I get to the stadium?
Ryan: Sorry, I don't know. I'm lost too!

HOW TO ❓
be polite

- Use 'Excuse me' to start a sentence.
- Use 'please' at the end of a sentence.
- Say 'Thank you' or 'Thanks'.

3 a Read the tips in the `HOW TO` box.

b ▶️▶️1.20 Watch or listen again and underline polite phrases in Exercise 2.

c ▶️1.21 Listen and repeat the questions.

4 a Match the directions (1–5) to the pictures (a–e).

1 Go straight on. ....
2 It's on the left. ....
3 Turn left. ....
4 Take the second right. ....
5 It's just round the corner. ....

  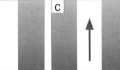

b ▶️1.22 Listen and repeat the sentences in Exercise 4a.

ACT

5 a 🔊 Student A: Ask for directions to these places. Repeat and check the directions.

cinema   museum   station   supermarket

Student B: Look at the map on page 141 and give your partner directions.

b 🔊 Student B: Ask for directions to these places. Repeat and check the directions.

castle   shopping centre   sports centre   zoo

Student A: Look at the map on page 141 and give your partner directions.

PHRASEBOOK ▶️1.23 📖

Ask for directions

Excuse me, ...

How do I get to ... ?

Can you tell me the way to ... , please?

I think I'm lost.

Thank you. / Thanks.

Give directions

Go straight on.

Turn left/right.

Take the first/second ... left/right.

It's on the left/right.

It's just round the corner.

You can't miss it.

⟩⟩⟩ Workbook, page 15

WRITING Hello from St Petersburg

>>> **Use correct punctuation**

SPEAK AND READ

1 **Work in pairs. Look at the title of the page and the photo. What do you know about this place?**

Dear Jessie,

Hello from St Petersburg! I love my city. It's got lots of beautiful parks and famous old buildings like the Hermitage Art Museum. Some people call St Petersburg 'Venice of the North' because of the city's rivers and canals. There's also a cool theme park, a water park and lots of great shops. Why don't you come and visit?

Best wishes,

Dasha

2 **Read the e-postcard. Tick (✓) the things Dasha writes about. Add two more things.**

a tower	old buildings
parks	a station
shops	rivers and canals
a castle	....
a museum	....

3 a **Read the tips in the (HOW TO) box.**

HOW TO

use correct punctuation

- Use capital letters to start a sentence and for names, cities and nationalities.
- Use full stops (.) at the end of sentences.
- Use commas (,) in lists or before new ideas.
- Use apostrophes (') for short forms of verbs and possessive *s*.
- Use question marks (?) at the end of questions.
- Add exclamation marks (!) for emphasis or instructions.

b **Find one example of each punctuation mark in Dasha's e-postcard.**

PRACTISE

4 **Add punctuation to Jessie's email.**

✉ New mail ← Reply → Forward

hi dasha
thanks for your e-postcard
st petersburg looks amazing in the cards photo
I can't speak russian do a lot of people speak english
write soon
jessie

Get it right

Start a postcard, email or letter to a friend with *Dear ...* or *Hi ...* .

Finish with *Best wishes, ... , Love, ...* or *Write soon!*

PLAN

5 **You're going to write an e-postcard from an interesting town or city. Use the *Writing plan* to help you prepare.**

WRITING PLAN

1 **Write a greeting and start your e-postcard.**

Where are you writing from?

2 **Write about the town or city.**

What special places has the city got?

What can you see?

What can you do?
(Use *have got* and *there is / there are*.)

3 **Finish your card and check your punctuation.**

WRITE AND CHECK

6 **Write your e-postcard. Then check it. Tick (✓) the things in the plan.**

SHARE

7 **Swap your e-postcard with other students. Say where you would like to go and why.**

VOCABULARY Places in a town

1 Complete the places.

My town is quite small …

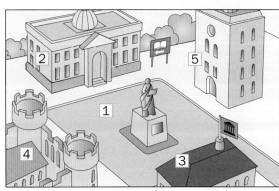

In the picture there is …
1 the s_____ e_____
2 the l_____ y
3 the art m_____ m
4 the c_____ e
5 the t_____ r

There isn't …
6 an ai_____ t
7 a train s_____ n
8 a sports s_____ m
9 sh_____ g c_____ e
10 a th_____ e p____ k

___ /10

MY
WORLD

Family

2 Complete the text with the family words in the two boxes.

… but my family is big!

| aunt | cousins | daughter | husband |
| parents | son | uncle | |

Mum and Dad are my (1) _____ , of course.
My (2) _____ Agatha is Dad's big sister.
Her (3) _____ is my (4) _____ Ron
(and also my history teacher!).
Helena is their (5) _____ and Travis is their
(6) _____ . They're my (7) _____ .

| granddaughter | grandparents | grandson |
| married | wife | |

Travis is (8) _____ to Scarlett, his
(9) _____ . They have a little girl – Agatha and
Ron's (10) _____ and a baby boy – Agatha and
Ron's (11) _____ . Agatha and Ron like being
(12) _____ .

___ /12

GRAMMAR *There is / there are*; prepositions of place

3 Choose the correct word or phrase.

Our favourite place is Paolo's Pizza Place.
(1) *There aren't / There isn't* a café in my town but
(2) *there's / there isn't* a good pizza restaurant.
(3) *There are / There's* lots of pizzas on the menu in
Paolo's Pizza Place. You can sit outside – (4) *there
aren't / there are* tables and chairs in the garden
(5) *under / behind* the restaurant. (6) And *there's /
there isn't* often music in the square (7) *over / next
to* Paolo's Pizza Place, so it's quite noisy!

___ /14

Have got

4 Complete with the correct form of *have got*.

My family loves gadgets!
My parents (1) _____ a lot of computers
and phones. But they aren't music fans, so they
(2) _____ music players.
I (3) _____ a computer (I want one!) but I
(4) _____ a phone.
My brother (5) _____ a tablet and a music
player. But he (6) _____ a phone so I can't
call him.
What gadgets (7) _____ you
_____ ?

___ /14

Your score: ___ /50

SKILLS CHECK

✓✓✓	Yes, I can. No problem!
✓✓	Yes, I can. But I need a bit of help.
✓	Yes, I can. But I need a lot of help.

I can identify the type of text. _____
I can listen for the main ideas. _____
I can understand different ways to say 'hello'. _____
I can ask for and give directions. _____
I can use correct punctuation. _____

NIGHT AND DAY

IN THE PICTURE Around the world

>>> Talk about your daily routine

WORK WITH WORDS Daily activities

1 a **RECALL** **Work in pairs. Say the times on the clocks. Use the words in the box.**

| half | o'clock | past | quarter | to |

1   2   3   4   5   6

b **Tell your partner when you do these things.**

| finish school | get up | go to bed | go to school | have lunch |

I finish school at 4 o'clock.

2 a **Work in pairs. Look at the photo. What can you see? Why are some countries light and other countries dark?**

b **Match the photos (a–d) to the messages (1–4). Which activity in bold can you see in each photo?**

c **Match the other activities in bold in the messages to the pictures (1–6) below.**

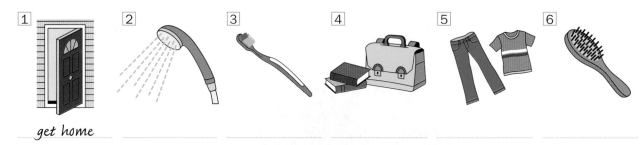

1 *get home*   2   3   4   5   6

3 ▶1.24 **Listen and repeat all the daily activities in bold in the messages.**

1
I **wake up** at 7am and **have a shower**. Then I **get dressed** and **brush my hair**.

2
I **have breakfast**, then I **pack my bag** and walk to school. I **get to school** at 8am.

PHRASE BYTES

The photo shows …

Some countries are light because …

3 I **do my homework** and at 7pm we have dinner. At 10pm I **clean my teeth** and go to bed.

4 I finish school at 3pm. I **go home** by bus and I **get home** at 3.45.

4 a Complete the sentences with *before* **or** *after*.

People normally …
1 get up _____ they wake up.
2 have a shower _____ they get dressed.
3 brush their hair _____ they have a shower.
4 go home _____ they get home.
5 clean their teeth _____ they have dinner.
6 do their homework _____ they go to school.

b Compare your answers with a partner. Are they the same? If not, why not?

5 THE MOVING PICTURE ▶ Watch the video. When the clocks stop, listen. Where's the boy or girl from?

SPEAK

6 Work in pairs. Compare your daily activities. Find three differences between your routines.

PHRASE BYTES

I wake up at … and then I …

Then/Next I …

Really? I … before/after I …

That's the first/second/third difference.

GO BEYOND

Do the Words & Beyond exercise on page 131.

READING Midnight sun

SPEAK AND READ

1 a 🔊 **Work in pairs. Look at the photos. Where do you think the town of Tromsø is?**

b Read the first lines of the school blog message. Check your answer to Exercise 1a.

2 a Read the tips in the HOW TO box.

b ▶1.25 Read the text quickly and complete the sentences about Tromsø.

1 Tromsø's _____ the Arctic Circle.
2 For _____ days a year, the sun shines for 24 hours a day.
3 June 23rd is called _____ .
4 In winter it's sometimes _____ for 24 hours.
5 A good time to see the Northern Lights is in _____ .
6 People have dinner at _____ .

PHRASE BYTES

I think it's in …

Maybe it's in … because …

There's a lot of snow, so it's …

HOW TO ❓

find specific information

☐ Don't read every sentence.

☐ Decide which words are important in the information that you need.

☐ Find the important words in the text.

☐ Read the sentences with the important words first.

TROMSØ

THE NORTHERN LIGHTS

| Home | About | New posts | Archive |

Hi to our new friends in Austin, Texas. Here's a description of life in Tromsø.

Tromsø is in the north of Norway. It's above the Arctic Circle, so there are 60 days in the summer when the sun shines 24 hours a day. On June 23rd we celebrate Midsummer's Eve. We go to the beach and have a barbecue. At midnight the beach is full of people!
In winter there are 60 days when it's dark all day and night. It snows a lot and it's really cold. But if you stay at home you feel tired and sad, so people go out. We play in the snow every day and go to a café or the cinema at the weekend. Winter's a good time to see the Northern Lights.

Schooldays are the same all year. School starts at 8.30 and we have lunch at 11.00. At 2.15 we go home and do homework. We have dinner at 4.30. In the evening we see our friends.

3 Which tips in the HOW TO box did you use for help with Exercise 2b? Tick (✓) them.

4 a Find three differences between daily activities in Tromsø and your daily activities. Write about your activities.

Tromsø: In winter they play in the snow every day.
Here: We play in the snow two or three days a year.

b Work in pairs. Compare your sentences. Are they the same?

PHRASE BYTES

I (don't) think Tromsø's a good place to live because …

I want to see / go to / play …

REACT

5 🔊 **Work in pairs. What do you think? Tell your partner.**

1 Is Tromsø a good place to live? Why?/Why not?
2 What things in Tromsø do you want to see or do?

GO BEYOND

Find prepositions of place in the blog message. Make a list: *in + Austin/ Tromsø/…* , etc.

>>> Talk about when you do things

READ >>> Grammar in context

1 Read the description. In what two ways are Auckland and Seville different?

My pen pal

Auckland (my city)

I live in Auckland in New Zealand and my pen pal lives in Seville in Spain. The time difference is 12 hours, so she goes to bed when my first lesson finishes and she studies when I'm asleep. We talk at the weekend. I call her on Sunday at 9 o'clock in the morning when it's 9 o'clock at night for her. The seasons are different too. Summer starts in December here. There, it starts in June.

Seville in Spain

STUDY

2 Complete the explanations with examples from Exercise 1.

Present simple positive

Use: For things that are generally true.
Summer _____ in December.

For habits and routines.
We _____ at the weekend.

Form:

Positive
I/you/we/they + verb
he/she/it + verb + -s*

*Spelling
-ch/-s/-sh/-x/-o + -es: *finish > finishes, go > goes*
-consonant-y + -ies: *study > studies*

3 Complete the explanations with *at*, *in* and *on*. Use Exercise 1 to help you.

Prepositions of time

Use and form:

_____ + days and dates
_____ + months, years, seasons (*summer*, etc), *the morning*, *the afternoon*, *the evening*
_____ + *night, midnight, lunchtime, the weekend*, the time (*6 o'clock*, etc)
See GRAMMAR DATABASE, page 121.

PRACTISE

4 Complete the description with the present simple form of the verbs.

My country

My name's Arzan and I (1) __*live*__ (live) in Addu City in the Maldives. People (2) _____ (fly) here from around the world for their holidays. The equator (3) _____ (cross) the Maldives, so the temperature (4) _____ (stay) at about 30°C all day. Days are very regular too. In Addu City the sun always (5) _____ (come) up and (6) _____ (go) down at 6 o'clock. There are two main seasons. From December to March we (7) _____ (get) dry weather, and from May to November it's windy and some days it (8) _____ (rain).

5 Complete the description with *at*, *in* and *on*.

My week

My name's Carmen and I come from Seville in Spain. School starts (1) __*in*__ September and we have long holidays (2) _____ the summer (July and August). This is a typical week during the school year. It starts (3) _____ Monday. I get up (4) _____ 7.15 and get ready for school. School starts (5) _____ 8.30. I have four or five classes (6) _____ the morning. (7) _____ lunchtime I stay at school. (8) _____ the afternoon I have one or two more classes. We have dinner (9) _____ 8 o'clock because that's when my parents get home. (10) _____ the weekend I see my friends and relax.

6 a ▶1.26 PRONOUNCE Listen and circle the verbs with an /ɪz/ sound at the end.

brushes	does	lives	plays	relaxes
starts	uses	watches		

b ▶1.27 Read the explanation. Then listen again and repeat the verbs above.

If the verb ends in *-ches*, *-ses*, *-shes* or *-xes*, pronounce /ɪz/ at the end.

WRITE AND SPEAK

7 a Work in pairs. Make notes for a video message about your country, town/city and daily life.

b Practise your video message. Then present it to other students.

LISTENING AND VOCABULARY Let me show you round

SPEAK AND LISTEN

1 **RECALL** **Work in pairs. Make a list of the rooms in a house.**

2 a **Read the tips in the HOW TO box.**

b **1.28 Listen to Matthew talking about his house. What's in each room? Write one letter from a–h next to each room (1–5).**

1	his bedroom	a	a vacuum cleaner
2	the bathroom	b	toys
3	his sister's room	c	Matthew's father
4	the living room	d	his sister
5	the kitchen	e	lunch
		f	musical instruments
		g	Matthew's parents
		h	a cat

3 **Which tips in the HOW TO box did you use for help with Exercise 2b? Tick (✓) them.**

4 **1.28 Listen again. Match the two parts of the sentences.**

1 Matthew   a have a big room.
2 His mum   b has an untidy room.
3 His dad   c has a lot of space for things.
4 His sister   d always sits in the armchair.
5 His parents   e always sits on the sofa.
6 Matthew   f normally cooks.

REACT

5 **Work in pairs. Compare your home with Matthew's house. What's similar? What's different?**

WORK WITH WORDS Furniture and other things in the home

6 a **Match the photos (1–12) to the words in the box.**

armchair	bookcase	carpet
cooker	cupboard	curtains
fridge	lamp	shelf (shelves)
sofa	wardrobe	washing machine

b **1.29 Amanda's describing her flat. Listen and check or complete your answers. She says the words in the same order as the photos.**

7 **1.30 Listen and repeat the words.**

8 **Think of a room in your house. Tell your partner what you can see in it. Can your partner guess the room?**

bathroom	bedroom	dining room
kitchen	living room	

I can see …
 Is it a/the … ?
That's right.
 No, it isn't.

GO BEYOND

Do the Words & Beyond exercises on page 131.

HOW TO
use sounds to help you understand

☐ Identify sounds. What can you hear?

☐ Use sounds to decide where people are.

☐ Use sounds to help with vocabulary.

GRAMMAR Present simple with adverbs of frequency

>>> **Talk about how often you do things**

READ >>> Grammar in context

1 Read the description. Are the two sisters friends?

My sister and I are twins, but we're very different. Carla **always** gets up late, so she's late for school every day. And she can **never** remember where her things are. She **hardly ever** brushes her hair (maybe once a week), and her room's **normally** in a mess (until Mum and Dad get angry). But we're good friends and we **often** do things together.

STUDY

2 Complete the explanations. Use Exercise 1 to help you.

always   hardly ever   never   normally

Present simple with adverbs of frequency

Use: To say how often you do things.

0%

sometimes

often

usually,

100%

Word order
adverb + main verb (*go, see*)
Karl always gets up late.
am/are/is/can + adverb
His room's always in a mess.
See GRAMMAR DATABASE, page 121.

PRACTISE

3 Complete the sentences with the adverbs of frequency in Exercise 2. Use the frequencies (0–100%) to help you.

1 I _____*never*_____ get up late. (0%)
2 I _____ eat fruit after dinner. (85%)
3 My school report is _____ perfect. (100%)
4 I _____ read before I go to bed. (30%)
5 I _____ help in the kitchen. (60%)
6 My parents are _____ angry with me. (5%)

4 Put the words in order to make sentences.

1 the morning / tired / is / in / Carla / usually
   Carla's usually tired in the morning.
2 often / her / She / homework / forgets

3 eats / ever / vegetables / hardly / She

4 her phone / She / find / never / can

5 on the sofa / sometimes / She / sleeps

6 happy / is / She / always

5 a Add an adverb of frequency to each sentence to make it true for you.

1 My bedroom is in a mess.
2 I have a shower in the morning.
3 I'm late for school.
4 I do my homework on the sofa.
5 I can do my English homework.
6 I watch TV in the evening.

b Work in pairs. Compare your answers.

How often is/are … ?

How often do you … ?

How often can you … ?

SPEAK

6 a Write three questions with *How often … ?* to ask other students.

b Ask three other students your questions. Write their answers.

c Tell the class one interesting thing.

Dasha often …

Mario can never …

LANGUAGE &BEYOND

'My room's quite untidy but I know where things are.' **Ida**

'My room's really organised. Everything has a place.' **Kara**

'My room's really untidy. I can never find things.' **Dean**

>>> Organise your things

GET ORGANISED

READ

1 **Work in pairs. Match the teenagers to their bedrooms (1–3). Who are you like?**

DO

2 **Work in pairs. Put the steps for organising your bedroom in the correct order.**

3 a **You decide to organise or reorganise your room. Follow the steps in Exercise 2. Then draw a simple plan of your room.**

b **Work in pairs. Show your plans. Explain where things are and why.**

> My books are next to my bed because I always read in bed.

> My CDs are in boxes because I never play them.

REFLECT

4 **Talk about the questions. Then read the REFLECTION POINT.**
 1 Why is it a good idea to organise your things?
 2 Do the five steps in Exercise 2 work. Why?/Why not?
 3 What other ways are there to organise your things?

EXTEND

5 **Decide how to organise or reorganise your classroom or another room in your school or house.**

(RE)ORGANISE YOUR THINGS!

___ PLAN: Decide where to put things you want to keep.

___ FINISH: Put things in their new place. Give the bag to another kid.

_1_ GET READY: Find some boxes, labels and a big bag.

___ CHOOSE: Make decisions about your things.
 1 *I use this.* > Don't touch it.
 2 *I want this but I hardly ever use it.* > Put it in a box. Add a label.
 3 *I don't want this.* > Put it in the bag.

___ START: Put your things on your bed. Put similar things together.

REFLECTION POINT

If you organise your things, it's easy to find them. You also make space for new things. But it's important to find a way to organise things that works for you.

>>> Ask for and tell the time when you travel

SPEAK

1 Work in pairs. Answer the questions.

1 When do you travel on buses and trains? Where do you go?
2 Bus and train timetables use the 24-hour clock. How do you say these times: *16:30, 19:05?*

WATCH OR LISTEN

2 ▶ ▶1.31 Watch or listen to the scenes. What do the people do next?

> **1**
> **May:** Excuse me. (1) _____ the next train to Oxford?
> **Guard:** Well, there's a fast one at 17:45.
> **May:** Seventeen forty-five. Sorry, (2) _____ is it now?
> **Guard:** It's 20 past five.
> **May:** Thanks. … Have we got time for a snack?
> **Alex:** Er … yes. We've got 25 minutes.
> **May:** Good. I'm really hungry.
>
> **2**
> **Joe:** Excuse me. (3) _____ the next bus to the sports centre?
> **Woman:** Um … I think it's at 13:05 but check on the timetable.
> **Joe:** Thanks. … (4) _____ the time now?
> **Adam:** It's half past 12.
> **Joe:** (5) _____ have we got till it goes?
> **Adam:** Thirty-five minutes.
> **Joe:** Let's walk. It's only 15 minutes on foot.

3 ▶ ▶1.31 Watch or listen again and complete the conversations.

4 ▶1.32 Listen and repeat the questions.

5 a Read the tips in the HOW TO box.

b Underline examples of making time to think in the conversations.

6 a ▶1.33 Listen and draw the time on the clocks.

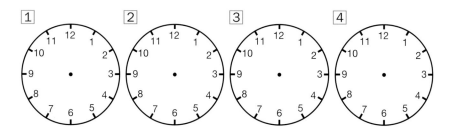

b ▶1.34 Work in pairs. Say the times in Exercise 6a in two or three different ways. Then listen and repeat all the times.

ACT

7 ⊙ In groups of four, practise two travel conversations. Then present your conversations to other groups.

Students A and C: Look at page 141.

Students B and D: Look at page 142.

>>> Workbook, page 27

HOW TO

make time to think

- Don't stop talking.

- Say *Well, … , Er …* or *Um …* before your sentence.

PHRASEBOOK ▶1.35

Ask for and tell the time

What's the time? / What time is it?

What time's the next … ?

When's the next … ?

There's one at …

(I think) it's at …

thirteen oh five = five past one

seventeen forty-five = quarter to six

How long have we got till it goes?

Make time to think

Well, …

Er …

Um …

WRITING My favourite room

>>> Use *also* and *too*

SPEAK AND READ

1 Work in pairs. Answer the questions.

Do you have a pen pal or friend in another country?
– If so, where does he/she live? What do you write about?
– If not, do you want a pen pal? Why?/Why not?

2 Read Judy's message to her pen pal. What's her favourite room?

Hi Ingrid!
I'm writing to you from my favourite room.
I love this room. It's got a big table in it and it also gets lots of light. I usually do my hotmework here because it's normally quiet too. It's also really warm because the cooker's next to the table. I can send a photo if you want.
See you soon!
Judy

HOW TO ?

use *also* and *too*

■ Use *also* and *too* to add another fact.

■ Use *also* after *be* and *have* in *have got* and before other verbs.

■ Use *too* at the end of a sentence.

3 a Read the tips in the HOW TO box.

b Underline examples of *also* and *too* in the message in Exercise 2.

PRACTISE

4 Complete the description with *also* and *too*.

9.30am

This is my bedroom. It's my sister's room
(1) _____ . It's never quiet because she listens to music all the time. She (2) _____ plays the guitar. But it's quite big. There's a wardrobe and there are some cupboards (3) _____ ,
so there's space for all our things. There's
(4) _____ a desk but I normally study in the kitchen!

PLAN

5 You're going to write a description for a pen pal of your favourite room. Use the *Writing plan* to help you prepare.

WRITING PLAN

1 **Say why it's your favourite room.** ▢
Why do you like it?

2 **Say what's in the room.** ▢
What furniture is there?

3 **Say what you normally do in it.** ▢
Do you study there? Watch TV? … ?

4 **Use *too* and *also* in your description.** ▢
Look at the tips in the HOW TO box.

WRITE AND CHECK

6 Write your description. Then check it. Tick (✓) the things in the plan.

SHARE

7 Swap your description with other students. Which room do most students choose as their favourite room?

>>> Workbook, pages 28–29

VOCABULARY Daily activities

1 Mike is British but lives in another country now. Complete his blog for his friends with the verbs in the box.

brush	clean	do	get (x3)	go	have
pack	wake				

MY NEW ROUTINE
Some things are really different here. I
(1) _____ up at 6am now but stay in bed
for 15 minutes. Then I get up, (2) _____ a
shower, (3) _____ dressed, (4) _____
my hair, have breakfast and (5) _____ my
teeth. I (6) _____ to school at 8am, but I
finish at 2pm and I can (7) _____ home.
When I (8) _____ home I (9) _____ my
homework, then I (10) _____ my bag for the
next day. Then I'm free to do other things!

___ /10

Furniture and other things in the home

2 Complete the words in Mike's blog.

MY NEW HOME
We live in a flat now, not a house. In my room
there's a small (1) wa_____ for
my clothes, a (2) bo_____ for my
books and lots of (3) sh_____ on the
wall. I need a new (4) cu_____
for my other things. There's also a big
(5) ca_____ on the floor and a
(6) la_____ for reading next to the bed. There
are no (7) cu_____ on the
window. In the living room there's a (8) so_____
and an (9) ar_____ , but they're
very old. The kitchen's got the usual things – a
(10) co_____ , (11) fr_____ and
(12) a wa_____ ma_____ .
But no dishwasher, so we wash the dishes
by hand.

___ /12

GRAMMAR Present simple positive; prepositions of time

3 Complete the blog with the correct form of the verbs or with *at*, *in* and *on*.

SCHOOL
The schoolday is different here. It (1) _____
(start) early but it (2) _____ (finish) early
too. Other things are the same. We have four
or five classes (3) _____ the morning, and
then there's a break for lunch. (4) _____
lunchtime most people (5) _____ (eat) in the
school canteen. The food's OK. (6) _____
Wednesdays my class (7) _____ (do) sport
after lunch. I (8) _____ (play) basketball. It's
a new sport for me but I really like it.

___ /16

Present simple with adverbs of frequency

4 Write complete sentences with the adverbs of frequency in the box.

always	hardly ever	never	often
sometimes	usually		

WEEKENDS
Here's what happens at the weekend.
1 I / get up / late. (**100%**)
2 We / go / shopping. (**80%**)
3 I / watch / a film with friends. (**60%**)
4 We / have / lunch with my parents' friends.
   (**30%**)
5 I / forget / to do my homework. (**5%**) ___
6 I / get / bored. (**0%**) ___ /12

Your score: ___ /50

SKILLS CHECK

✓✓✓ Yes, I can. No problem!
✓✓   Yes, I can. But I need a bit of help.
✓   Yes, I can. But I need a lot of help.

I can find specific information when I read.
I can use sounds to help me understand.
I can organise my things.
I can ask for and tell the time when I travel.
I can use *also* and *too* when I write.

READ

1 Read the sentences about Melissa's hometown. Choose the best word (A, B or C) for each space.

Example:

0 My hometown's ___*between*___ two big rivers.

   A under   B behind   Ⓒ between

---

1 I love my hometown because _____ are a lot of things to see and do there.

   A we   B there   C it

2 Tourists always come to visit the square _____ the centre of the city.

   A in   B over   C on

3 The main library's in the square. I often go there to _____ video games and CDs to play at home.

   A sell   B use   C get

4 There's a big shopping centre _____ to the library where I sometimes meet friends.

   A in front   B next   C across

5 The town's _____ got a famous castle which is now a natural history museum.

   A too   B has   C also

Reading: _____ /10

EXAM TIPS

 complete sentences with multiple-choice answers

- Look at the example. It shows you what to do.

- Read each sentence and the word choices.

- Decide which words are definitely wrong. For each word choice, ask:
  - Does it have the correct meaning?
  - Can you use it with the words before and after it?

- Read the sentence again and check your answer.

LISTEN

2 ▶1.36 **Listen to five conversations. You will hear each conversation twice. Choose the correct answer for each question (A, B or C).**

Example:

0 What's Charlie's first activity in the morning?

1 Which is Susan's room?

2 What time does the boys' train leave?

3 Where's the noise from?

4 Which is the right note?

A Monday, 7pm Mark's house

B Tuesday, 7pm Mark's house

C Wednesday, 7pm, Mark's house

5 Which is the right station?

Listening: _____ /10

WRITE

3 **Read the descriptions and complete the family words.**

Example:

0 The word for a person's child (a boy, not a girl). s *o n*

1 They're a person's mum or dad.   p _____
2 She's your mum or dad's sister.   a _____
3 If two people are married, the man is this.   h _____
4 The word for a person's child (a girl, not a boy).   d _____
5 It's your mum or dad's father.   g _____

_____ /5

4 **Read the email from your pen friend, Kim. Write an email to Kim and answer the questions (25–35 words).**

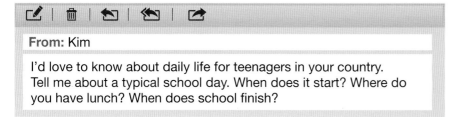

From: Kim

I'd love to know about daily life for teenagers in your country. Tell me about a typical school day. When does it start? Where do you have lunch? When does school finish?

_____ /5

Writing: _____ /10

Progress check score _____ /30

EXAM TIPS ✓

❓ answer multiple choice questions with pictures

- Read the questions before you listen.
- Look at the pictures: what English words and numbers can you see?
- Listen for these words and numbers. What do the speakers say about them?
- When you listen again, check your answers.

❓ listen for the main ideas
See page 14

❓ use sounds to help you understand
See page 24

❓ make time to think
See page 27

EXAM TIPS ✓

❓ complete words from descriptions

- Read the instructions carefully.
- Read the description and the first letter. Can you think of the word?
- Check your word has the correct number of letters. (One space is one letter.)
- Check that your spelling of the word is correct.

EXAM TIPS ✓

❓ reply to an email or message

- Read the email or message carefully.
- Write your reply. Answer all the questions in the email or message.
- Use the correct number of words. Count them.

❓ use correct punctuation
See page 18

UNIT 3 CLASSMATES

IN THE PICTURE School icons

>>> **Talk about school subjects**

WORK WITH WORDS School subjects

1 **RECALL** **Work in pairs. Write words for the different categories.**

five things you do at school: *answer questions, …*
four things you use in class: *an exercise book, …*
three things your teacher uses in class: *a board, …*
two things you see on the classroom wall: *a timetable, …*

2 **Match the icons (a–l) to the UK school subjects in the box. Which subject doesn't have an icon?**

art	design & technology	drama	English	geography
history	IT (information technology)	languages	maths	
music	PE (physical education)	science		

3 a ▶1.37 **Listen and check your answers to Exercise 2. Then listen and repeat.**

b **Create an icon for the missing subject in Exercise 2.**

4 ▶1.38 **Look at the timetable and complete the sentences below. Then listen and check.**

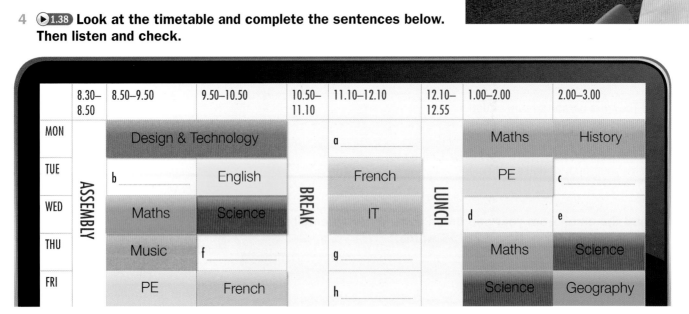

	8.30–8.50	8.50–9.50	9.50–10.50	10.50–11.10	11.10–12.10	12.10–12.55	1.00–2.00	2.00–3.00
MON	ASSEMBLY	Design & Technology		BREAK	a	LUNCH	Maths	History
TUE		b	English		French		PE	c
WED		Maths	Science		IT		d	e
THU		Music	f		g		Maths	Science
FRI		PE	French		h		Science	Geography

1 We have _____ on Monday, Wednesday and Thursday.
2 We do _____ on Tuesday afternoon and Friday morning.
3 We have our _____ class on Wednesday at 11.10.
4 On Thursday our first class is _____ .
5 We study _____ for two hours each week. I study French.
6 The week starts with two hours of _____ .

5 ▶1.39 **Listen and complete the timetable with the school subjects.**

6 **THE MOVING PICTURE** ▶ **Watch the video of four teenagers talking about school subjects. Which are their favourite subjects? Why?**

7 **Complete the sentences about your school timetable.**

1 My schoolday starts at _____ and ends at _____ .
2 We have a break at _____ .
3 My favourite school subject/s is/are _____ .
4 I like _____ but I don't like _____ .
5 I have English on _____ .
6 We do _____ at _____ on _____ .

SPEAK

8 **Work in pairs. Complete the tasks.**

1 Write sentences about three school subjects.
2 Read your sentences to your partner. Can your partner name the school subject?

We do it on Mondays and Wednesdays. We learn about important people and dates in the past.

Is it history?

GO BEYOND

Do the Words & Beyond exercise on page 132.

Workbook, page 32

READING An interview

SPEAK AND READ

1 Work in pairs. Answer the questions.

1 Is your school big or small?
2 How many teachers and students are there?
3 What do you like about the school?

2 a Read the tips in the HOW TO box.

b ▶1.40 **What does Jon talk about? Read the interview and tick (✓) the information.**

The building ☐   The number of students ☐   The timetable ☐
The teachers ☐   The subjects ☐   The school food ☐

HOW TO
understand the main ideas

☐ Read the text quickly.
☐ Don't try to understand every word.
☐ Think about the general topic.

MY SCHOOL RULES!

REPORTER: What's your name and where do you go to school?
JON: My name's Jon and I go to the Evelyn Grace Academy in Brixton, South London. I'm in Year 8.
REPORTER: Do you like it?
JON: Yes, I do. The school building's amazing. Every day we walk along a running track to go into the school.
REPORTER: Are there a lot of students?
JON: Yes, there are. There are around 800 students.
REPORTER: When do you start and finish school?
JON: We start at 8.30 in the morning. We finish at 3.15 but I usually don't get home until 5.30 because I have extra classes.

REPORTER: Do you get tired?
JON: No, I don't. Well, maybe sometimes. But the extra classes mean more dance and music. I like music a lot.
REPORTER: What subjects do you do?
JON: We do all the usual school subjects like science and history. Maths is my favourite subject. In Year 8 we do extra English and maths.
REPORTER: Are there any school rules?
JON: Yes, there are. We all wear a uniform. And we can't take phones inside the school.

3 Which tips in the HOW TO box did you use for help with Exercise 2b? Tick (✓) them.

4 Read the interview again and complete the reporter's notes.

5 Answer the questions.

1 How do students enter the Evelyn Grace Academy?
2 How often does Jon get tired?
3 Why does Jon like the extra classes?

REACT

6 ⬚ Work in pairs. What do you think? Tell your partner.

1 Describe the Evelyn Grace Academy building. Do you like it? Why?/Why not?
2 In what ways is the Evelyn Grace Academy different from your school?

STUDENT NAME:

YEAR:

N° STUDENTS:

SCHOOL TIMES:

FAVOURITE SUBJECT:

RULES:

PHRASE BYTES

I think the building looks …

It's very …

In our school … , but at the Evelyn Grace Academy …

GO BEYOND

In pairs, ask and answer the questions in the interview about *your* school.

>>> Use negative verbs and ask and answer questions

READ AND LISTEN >>> Grammar in context

1 ►1.41 **Read and listen to the interview. In what way is Bella's school different?**

Reporter: Where do you go to school?
Bella: I go to Watershed School in Colorado, USA.
Reporter: Do you like it?
Bella: Yes, I do.
Reporter: Do you think Watershed is a typical school?
Bella: No, I don't. We do the usual school subjects but we don't spend all day in classrooms.
Reporter: What do you do?
Bella: We go to local farms and organisations to learn in the real world. And we visit other countries.
Reporter: Does the school have classrooms?
Bella: Yes, it does. But the school doesn't believe you can learn everything in a classroom. At Watershed, the world is our classroom.

STUDY

2 **Complete the explanations with examples from Exercise 1.**

Present simple

Use: For habits, routines and things that are generally true.

Form:

Negative
don't/doesn't + verb
We _____ *all day in classrooms.*

Questions
do/does + *I/he*, etc + verb
Where _____ *to school?*
_____ *it?*

Short answers
Yes, I _____ *. / Yes, he does.*
No, I don't. / No, she doesn't.

See GRAMMAR DATABASE, page 122.

PRACTISE

3 a **Write the complete questions.**

1 Where / Bella / go to school?
Where does Bella go to school?
2 she / like / it?
3 she / think / her school is typical?
4 Why / she / think it's different?
5 How / they / learn in the real world?
6 What / Bella say / at the end?

b **Write answers to the questions. Use Exercise 1 to help you.**
1 She goes to Watershed School.

4 **Complete the text with the present simple form of the verbs.**

I (1) _____ (not go) to school.
My sister (2) _____ (not go) to school either. Our mum and dad are our teachers.
They (3) _____ (not work) in an office.
They work at home. But we (4) _____ (not spend) all day at home. We often go on study trips. My favourite subject is geography.
I (5) _____ (not like) history.
It (6) _____ (not interest) me.

5 **Complete the questions with the question words in the box. Use each word once. One question doesn't use a question word.**

How	What	When	Where	Which
Who	Why			

1 _____ do you travel to school?
2 _____ do you live?
3 _____ does the school day start and end?
4 _____ do you usually do after school?
5 _____ do you usually talk to in breaks?
6 _____ do you like (or not like) your school?
7 _____ does your school organise trips to other countries?
8 _____ school subjects don't interest you?

SPEAK

6 a **Work in pairs. Ask and answer the questions in Exercise 5.**

How do you travel to school?   *I usually go by bus.*

b **Tell the class two interesting facts about your partner.**

Cris travels to school by bus and she usually plays tennis after school.

SPEAK AND LISTEN

1 **RECALL** **Work in pairs. Answer the questions.**

1 Which of these clothes can you see in the photos?

| dress | jacket | jeans | shirt | shoes |
| skirt | socks | trainers | trousers | T-shirt |

2 Which of the clothes do you usually wear at school or at home?

2 ▶1.42 **Listen to three teenagers talk about their school uniforms. Match the names to the photos.**

1 Kath .... 2 Dani .... 3 Chloe ....

3 a **Read the tips in the HOW TO box.**

b ▶1.42 **Listen again and match the information to the correct photo (a–c).**

1 The uniform's quite traditional. ....
2 The students designed the uniform. ....
3 They have special clothes for sport. ....
4 Students can wear jewellery. ....
5 They have a school backpack. ....

4 **Which tips in the HOW TO box did you use for help with Exercise 3b? Tick (✓) them.**

HOW TO

listen for specific information

☐ Read the task carefully.

☐ Decide which words in the task are important.

☐ Listen carefully for this information.

REACT

5 **Work in pairs. Answer the questions.**

1 Which of the uniforms in Exercise 3b is your favourite?
2 Do you think school uniforms are a good thing? Why?/Why not?

WORK WITH WORDS Clothes and accessories

6 a **Match the pictures (a–l) to the words in the box.**

..... backpack	..... belt	..... coat	..... earrings	..... gloves
..... hoody	..... scarf	..... shorts	..... jumper	..... tie
..... tracksuit bottoms	..... tracksuit top

b ▶1.43 **Listen and check your answers. Listen again and repeat.**

7 ▶1.44 **PRONOUNCE** **Listen to the /əʊ/ sound in these words. Is it a short or long sound? Listen again and repeat.**

cl**o**thes   c**oa**t   ph**o**to   h**o**me   Chl**o**e

8 ▶1.45 **Complete the quotes with words from Exercise 6a. Then listen and check.**

1 'We can wear jewellery too, like _____.'
2 'We have a school _____ to carry stuff.'
3 'We have blue _____ and bottoms for outside sports.'
4 'We wear a grey jumper, a school scarf, gloves and a _____ to keep warm.'
5 'We wear our normal clothes like Sam's skateboard _____.'
6 'I forgot the school _____. It's got stripes.'

9 **Work in pairs. Design a school uniform for your school. What clothes and colours would you choose?**

GO BEYOND

Do the Words & Beyond exercise on page 132.

GRAMMAR Possessive 's, *whose* and possessive pronouns

>>> Talk about possessions and relationships

READ AND LISTEN >>> Grammar in context

1 ▶1.46 **Read and listen to the conversation. Who does the coat belong to?**

When the teacher arrives, the students' things are all on the floor.

Mr Ford: This changing room is a mess. Whose things are these? Are they all yours?

Todd: They aren't *all* ours, sir.

Mr Ford: Whose tracksuit top is this?

Martin: It's mine, sir.

Mr Ford: And these trainers?

Todd: They're Harry's trainers, I think.

Mr Ford: Who's Harry?

Martin: Harry is Todd's brother, sir.

Mr Ford: And this coat? Is it Harry's?

Todd: No, sir. It's yours.

STUDY

2 **Complete the explanations with examples from Exercise 1.**

Possessive 's and *whose*

Use: To talk about possessions or relationships.

Form:
noun + 's
The trainers belong to Harry. → *They're Harry's (trainers).*
Harry is the brother of Todd. → *Harry is*

_____ .
regular plural noun + s'
The _____ *things are all on the floor.*

Questions
Whose + noun + question
_____ *tracksuit top is this?*
See GRAMMAR DATABASE, page 122.

3 **Read the explanation and complete the table with possessive pronouns. Use Exercise 1 to help you.**

Possessive pronouns

Use: In place of a possessive adjective (*my*, *your*) + noun.

Form:
It's my tracksuit top. → *It's mine.*
It's your coat. → *It's yours.*

Possessive adjectives	Possessive pronouns
my	
your	
his/her	*his/hers*
our	
their	*theirs*

See GRAMMAR DATABASE, page 122.

PRACTISE

4 **Complete the sentences with the words in brackets. Add an apostrophe (') in the correct place.**

1 These are _____ gloves. (Dan)
2 This is _____ room. (my parents)
3 That's _____ school over there. (Chloe)
4 Those are _____ cats. (our neighbours)
5 I really like _____ earrings. (Kath)
6 This is _____ changing room. (the students)

5 ▶1.47 **Complete the conversation with the words in the box. Then listen and check.**

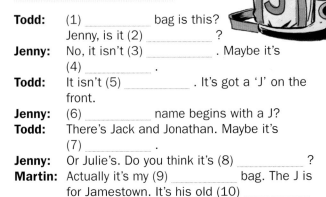

brother's	hers	
his	Martin's	mine
school's	theirs	
whose (x2)	yours	

Todd: (1) _____ bag is this? Jenny, is it (2) _____ ?

Jenny: No, it isn't (3) _____ . Maybe it's (4) _____ .

Todd: It isn't (5) _____ . It's got a 'J' on the front.

Jenny: (6) _____ name begins with a J?

Todd: There's Jack and Jonathan. Maybe it's (7) _____ .

Jenny: Or Julie's. Do you think it's (8) _____ ?

Martin: Actually it's my (9) _____ bag. The J is for Jamestown. It's his old (10) _____ name.

SPEAK

6 **Work in pairs. Do the tasks.**

1 Find several objects: your possessions, your partner's possessions or another student's possessions.

2 Write short sentences about each object.
   EXAMPLE: *Object 1 is Juan's red exercise book.*

3 Show your objects to another pair. Can they identify the correct person?

Whose red exercise book is this?

No, it isn't. It's Juan's.

I think it's Sylvia's exercise book.

LANGUAGE BEYOND

>>> **Understand your learning style**

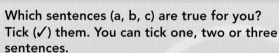

LEARNING STYLES

Which sentences (a, b, c) are true for you? Tick (✓) them. You can tick one, two or three sentences.

In class …
a I prefer to listen to explanations.
b I prefer to read explanations.
c I prefer to do an activity to understand an explanation.

Out of class …
a I often tell jokes and stories.
b I'm good at taking photos.
c I like to make things with my hands.

READ AND LISTEN

1 a **Read the website article and follow the instructions.**

   b ▶1.48 **Now read and listen. What type of learner are you? (You can have more than one style.)**

2 ☺ **Work in pairs. Talk about Exercise 1. Do you agree with the website article?**

DO

3 **Look at these typical classroom activities. Tick (✓) the activities you like.**

   ☐ Reading   ☐ Listening   ☐ Speaking
   ☐ Pronunciation   ☐ Project work   ☐ Role-play

4 ☺ **Work in pairs. Are the activities in Exercise 3 good for (a) auditory, (b) visual or (c) kinaesthetic learners? Explain why.**

REFLECT

5 **Talk about the questions. Then read the** **REFLECTION POINT**.
   1 Why are the students in the photo different colours?
   2 Do you think the other students in your class have the same learning style as you? Why?/Why not?
   3 How can it help you in class if you know your learning style?

EXTEND

6 **People with different learning styles are often good at different things. In groups, ask questions to find out what each person in the group is good at. Do the results match that person's learning style?**

   Are you good at playing football?

   Yes, I am. / No, I'm not.

There are three main types of learning styles:
a *auditory* learners like to hear information.
b *visual* learners like to see things.
c *kinaesthetic* learners like to do things to help them learn.

PHRASE BYTES

The article says I'm a(n) …

I think that's true.

I don't agree. I think I'm a(n) …

PHRASE BYTES

I think reading activities are good for … learners because …

REFLECTION POINT

Your learning style is the way you learn things. If you know your learning style, you can use it to help you understand and remember things.

38

SPEAK

1 a Work in pairs. Think of two words or phrases to complete the sentences.

1 She plays ... *tennis. / the violin.*
2 She always wears ...
3 He loves ...
4 He's got ... eyes.
5 She's got ... hair.
6 He's ...

b Compare your sentences with other students.

WATCH OR LISTEN

2 ▶▶1.49 Watch or listen to the scene. Write the names under the four correct photos opposite.

Claire Salva Manu Emma

Liz: Here's the list of students for the school play.
Adam: Ah, thanks. Who's Claire?
Liz: You know her.
Adam: No, I don't. What's she like?
Liz: Er, she's got long, wavy hair ... and she's got brown eyes. She always wears (1) _____ and she plays (2) _____ .
Adam: Ah, right. What about Salva? Is he the tall Italian guy?
Liz: No. He isn't very tall. And he isn't Italian. He's (3) _____ . He's got big brown eyes. He loves (4) _____ .
Adam: And Manu and Emma?
Liz: They're friends. He's tall and wears glasses. She's got (5) _____ blonde hair. He's got dark hair. He's (6) _____ .
Adam: OK. Let's see if they can act.

3 ▶▶1.49 Watch or listen again. Complete the conversation with the missing words.

4 ▶1.50 Match the sentence halves. Then listen and check your answers.

1 He's   a plays tennis.
2 She's got   b music.
3 His   c young.
4 She sometimes   d brother's name is Pep.
5 He likes   e straight, dark hair.

5 Write five sentences to describe the two other people in the photos.

He's got short straight hair.

ACT

6 ⬤ Work in groups of three or four. Complete the tasks.

1 Choose two people in the class.
2 Think about how to describe the people.
3 Take it in turns to say your descriptions to the class. Can the other students identify the people?

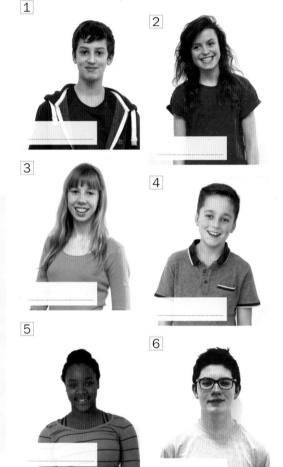

1 2 3 4 5 6

PHRASEBOOK ▶1.51

Describe appearance and nationality
He's/She's ...
tall/old/young/Spanish.

Describe hair and eyes
He's/She's got ...
black/blonde/brown/grey/dark hair.
long/short/wavy/straight hair.
brown/green/blue eyes.

Describe clothes and activities
He/She ...
plays the guitar / wears glasses / wears T-shirts / likes/loves sport.

WRITING A questionnaire

>>> Use *and*, *or* and *but*

SPEAK AND READ

1 **Work in pairs. Complete the tasks.**

1 Ask and answer the questions in the class questionnaire. Write your partner's answers.

2 Compare your answers with other students in the class. Are your answers similar?

CLASSMATES – *THINGS WE DO AND LIKE*
Read the **four** questions and write your answers.

1 Which is your favourite school subject – English, maths or geography?

2 How often do you go to the cinema – never, sometimes or often?

3 Pop, rock and classical are all types of music. Which do you prefer?

4 It's Saturday afternoon. You want to go out but it's raining. What do you do?

2 a **Read the tips in the `HOW TO` box.**

HOW TO ?

use *and*, *or* and *but*

- Use *and* to add another similar idea.
- Use *or* to add a choice.
- Use *but* to add a different idea.
- In a list, *and/or* usually come before the last word or phrase.

b **Underline examples of *and*, *or* and *but* in the questionnaire in Exercise 1.**

PRACTISE

3 **Complete the sentences with *and*, *or* or *but*. Use the `HOW TO` box to help you.**

1 My favourite subjects are history .... science.

2 I like rock music .... I don't like classical music.

3 I usually have a glass of orange .... apple juice for breakfast.

4 I want to watch the film on TV tonight .... it starts very late.

5 My brother can speak German, Spanish .... French.

6 After school we can go to the park and play football, ... we can go home and watch TV.

PLAN

4 **You're going to write a questionnaire about things you and your classmates do and like. Use the *Writing plan* to help you prepare.**

WRITING PLAN

1 **Think of different topics for your questions.**

What things do you like? Do you want to ask questions about school, sport, music, languages … ?

2 **Think of answer options.**

How many answer options do you want to give – two, three or four?

3 **Use *and*, *or* or *but* in your questions and answer options.**

Look at the tips in the `HOW TO` box.

WRITE AND CHECK

5 **Write four questions for your questionnaire. Include one situation (see question 4 in the questionnaire in Exercise 1). Then check it. Tick (✓) the things in the plan.**

SHARE

6 **Swap your questionnaire with other students. Write your answers to their questions. Then read their answers to your questionnaire.**

VOCABULARY School subjects

1 Complete the names of the school subjects.

> Welcome to the Lunar Secondary School website. Please follow the links to read about our school subjects.

> ★ LUNAR ★
> Secondary School

1. a _____
2. d _____ n & t _____ y
3. d _____ a
4. E _____ h
5. g _____ y
6. h _____ y
7. i _____ n t _____ y (IT)
8. l _____ s
9. m _____ s
10. m _____ c
11. p _____ l e _____ n (PE)
12. s _____ e

___ /12

Clothes and accessories

2 Write the names of the items.

> You can order your Lunar Secondary School uniform and accessories online.

1 _____
2 _____
3 _____
4 _____
5 _____
6 _____

7 _____
8 _____
9 _____
10 _____
11 _____
12 _____

___ /12

GRAMMAR Present simple negative, questions and short answers

3 Complete the questions and answers. Some are short answers.

Read an interview with our teacher, Mr Astro.

Reporter: (1) _____ (what / you / do)?
Mr Astro: I'm a teacher.
Reporter: (2) _____ (you / like) your job?
Mr Astro: (3) Yes, _____ .
Reporter: (4) _____ (why / you / think) Lunar School is different?
Mr Astro: A schoolday on planet Earth is about six hours. On the moon the schoolday (5) _____ (not finish) at the same time. A lunar day is very long.
Reporter: (6) _____ (students / wear) their own clothes?
Mr Astro: (7) No, _____ . They wear the special Lunar School uniform.
Reporter: (8) _____ (the students / enjoy) Lunar School?
Mr Astro: Let's go and ask them …

___ /16

Possessive 's and possessive pronouns

4 Complete the sentences with possessive 's and possessive pronouns.

Take a video tour of our school.
1 'This is our classroom. It's _____ .'
2 'And this is my desk. It's _____ .'
3 'Clare sits next to me. That's _____ desk.'
4 'These are Mr Astro _____ books. They're _____ .'
5 'This is the teachers _____ room. It's _____ .'
6 'That's my sister _____ coat. It's _____ .'
7 'And this video is for you. It's _____ .'

___ /10

Your score: ___ /50

SKILLS CHECK

✓✓✓ Yes, I can. No problem!
✓✓ Yes, I can. But I need a bit of help.
✓ Yes, I can. But I need a lot of help.

I can understand the main ideas when I read. _____
I can listen for specific information. _____
I can understand my learning style. _____
I can describe people. _____
I can use and, or and but when I write. _____

UNIT 4
WHAT'S GOING ON?

IN THE PICTURE Staying in and going out

>>> Talk about activities

a

WORK WITH WORDS Activity verbs

1 a **RECALL** **Work in pairs. Match words from the two boxes to make free-time activities. Use the photos to help you. You have one minute.**

go	listen	a bike	a book	to the cinema	football
meet	play	friends	shopping	swimming	television
read	ride	on the internet	to music	the piano	
watch		video games			

c

b **2.01 Listen and check.**

2 **Work in pairs. Use the activities in Exercise 1a to do the tasks.**

1 Student A: Make a list of the activities you stay in to do.
Student B: Make a list of the activities you go out to do.
2 Compare your lists. Are any activities on both lists?

3 **2.02 Complete the sentences with the verbs in the box. Then match the speakers (1–6) to the photos (a–f). Listen and check.**

go	laugh	leave	listen to	open	
put on	send	sit	start	stay in	

1 'At the festival people usually ＿＿＿＿＿ on the ground, relax
and ＿＿＿＿＿ the music.'
2 'The best part is waiting for the film to ＿＿＿＿＿.' ＿
3 'We chat and ＿＿＿＿＿ messages. If I'm on my own, I
＿＿＿＿＿ my headphones.'
4 'I never ＿＿＿＿＿ on Saturdays. I meet the other girls at the
funfair. We always ＿＿＿＿＿ a lot.'
5 'I usually ＿＿＿＿＿ into town by bus. At the bus stop I
＿＿＿＿＿ my book and read.'
6 'We watch the important matches on big TV screens. If we win, we're
happy when we ＿＿＿＿＿ but if we lose …'

e

4 a **Match the words below to verbs in Exercise 3 that have an opposite meaning.**

1 close _open_
2 come ＿＿＿
3 cry ＿＿＿
4 end ＿＿＿
5 go out ＿＿＿

6 arrive ＿＿＿
7 get ＿＿＿
8 stand ＿＿＿
9 take off ＿＿＿
10 talk to ＿＿＿

b **2.03 Listen and check your answers. Then listen and repeat.**

5 **THE MOVING PICTURE** ▶ **Watch the video. When does Holly usually go out and what does she do?**

6 Make notes about your typical weekend activities. Include verbs from Exercise 4a.

Friday evening: stay in, play video games, listen to music

FRIDAY PM: _____

SATURDAY AM: _____

SATURDAY PM: _____

SUNDAY AM: _____

SUNDAY PM: _____

SPEAK

7 Work in pairs. Ask and answer questions about a typical weekend. Use your notes from Exercise 6.

What do you usually do on Friday evening?

On Friday evening I usually stay in and play video games.

What do you do on Saturday morning/ afternoon/evening?

GO BEYOND

Do the Words & Beyond exercise on page 133.

READING Singing in the rain

SPEAK AND READ

1 **Work in pairs. Answer the questions.**

1 Which of these things do you read?
- blogs
- books
- comics
- magazines
- messages (phone/internet)
- newspapers

2 Which is your favourite thing to read? Why?

2 ▶2.04 **Read the text. How is it different from a text in a book or magazine?**

🏠 HOME   @ CONNECT   # DISCOVER

The dancers are closing their umbrellas, taking off their hats and going away. The song's ending. It's over. Wow!
5 seconds ago

What's happening now?   22 seconds ago

Yes. They're all smiling and laughing. Some of them are taking photos.   47 seconds ago

Are the people still watching?   1 minute ago

Wait! There are more performers. They're all wearing hats and carrying umbrellas. They're dancing and singing too.   1 minute ago

They're standing and watching. Someone's making a video.   1 minute ago

What are the people doing?   2 minutes ago

It's the 'Singing in the Rain/Umbrella' song from *Glee*. A woman's walking towards him. She's singing and now they're dancing to the music.   2 minutes ago

What's he singing?   2 minutes ago

No, it isn't raining! Wait! Now he's singing! I'm sending you a photo.   3 minutes ago

Is it raining?   3 minutes ago

A man's standing in the middle of the station floor. He's opening an umbrella.   3 minutes ago

Wait! Something's happening. There's music playing. People are looking around. Where's the music coming from? 😊?
4 minutes ago

Well, people are arriving or leaving by train. And some people are buying tickets. Others are looking at timetables.
4 minutes ago

Is anything happening?   5 minutes ago

I'm having a sandwich at the station café. 😊   5 minutes ago

Hi. What are you doing?   5 minutes ago

---

3 **a** **Read the tips in the HOW TO box.**

b **Put the events in the messages in the correct order.**

_____ The woman walks towards the man.
_____ The man opens an umbrella.
_____ The man and woman dance to the music.
_____ The dancers take off their hats.
_____ Music starts playing.
_____ People arrive and leave by train.

4 **Which tips in the HOW TO box did you use for help with Exercise 3b? Tick (✓) them.**

5 **Choose the correct description of the situation.**

A People are watching a video on a big screen at the rail station.
B A group of people are singing and dancing in a public place.
C A girl in a café is talking to a friend about a video on the internet.

REACT

6 💬 **Work in pairs. What do you think? Tell your partner.**

1 What kinds of videos are popular on the internet?
2 Would you like to be in a video like *Singing in the Rain*?

HOW TO ❓
understand the order of messages

☐ Read the message at the top. Is it the first message?

☐ Look for the first message. Use dates and/or times to help you.

☐ Read the messages in the correct order.

PHRASE BYTES 📖

Videos with animals … are very popular.

I'd like / I wouldn't like to be in a video because …

GO BEYOND

Write a description of your favourite video using 20–30 words.

READ AND LISTEN >>> Grammar in context

1 ▶2.05 **Read and listen to the phone conversation. Where do you think Louis is?**

Louis: Hi Ben. What are you doing?

Ben: Nothing much. I'm doing my homework. What about you?

Louis: Right now I'm standing in the middle of Times Square in New York with Mel. We're shopping, taking photos and having a fantastic time.

Ben: Are you telling the truth?

Louis: Yes, I am.

Ben: Is Mel listening to this conversation?

Louis: No, she isn't. Um … She's talking to some reporters at the moment. They're asking questions.

Ben: Listen, Louis. You aren't standing in Times Square and Mel isn't talking to reporters. You're telling one of your stories.

Louis: No, I'm not … OK. Yes, I am. I'm bored. Ben? What are you doing later?

Ben: I'm meeting Mel!

STUDY

2 **Complete the explanations with examples from Exercise 1.**

Present continuous

Use: For things in progress now or around now.

Form: Positive
be (I'm/you're, etc) + verb + -ing:
I _____ my homework.

Negative
be + not (I'm not/you aren't, etc) + verb + -ing:
Mel _____ to reporters.

Questions and short answers
be + I/you, etc + verb + -ing:
_____ the truth?
Yes, I am. / Yes, he is.
No, I'm not. / No, she isn't.

Time expressions: *now, right now,* _____

Present continuous for the future

Use: For arrangements at specific times in the future.
What are you doing later?
I _____ Mel.

Time expressions: *later, at six o'clock, next weekend*
See GRAMMAR DATABASE, page 123.

>>> Workbook, pages 46–47

PRACTISE

3 **Complete Louis' story with the present continuous form of the verbs.**

1 I *'m standing* (stand) in Camp Nou football stadium.
2 I _____ (play) with Barcelona Football Club.
3 The referee _____ (look) at his watch.
4 We _____ (play) in the final.
5 The other team _____ (not win); we are!
6 Now I _____ (run) with the ball. Goooooooooaaaaalllllll!!

4 **Write four sentences about another of Louis' stories.**

1 I'm sitting …

5 ▶2.06 (PRONOUNCE) **Listen to the /ŋ/ sound at the end of the verbs. Listen again and repeat.**

coming   going   talking   listening   running
walking   sitting   standing

6 a **Write the questions. Then write your answers to the questions. You can use short answers.**

1 What / you / do / at the moment?
2 Who / you / sit / next to?
3 your teacher / talk?
4 it / rain / outside?
5 you / meet friends / later?
6 What / you / do / next weekend?

b **Work in pairs. Ask and answer the questions.**

SPEAK

7 **Work in pairs. Look at the photos on pages 42 and 43 for 15 seconds. Close the book and describe what's happening in the photos. How much can you remember?**

People are sitting on the ground.

They're listening to music.

LISTENING AND VOCABULARY Soundscape

SPEAK AND LISTEN

1 Work in pairs. Look at the different types of audio. Where do you usually hear them?

- announcement
- conversation
- audio tour
- lesson (or talk)

You usually hear announcements in a station.

Or in a big shop.

HOW TO ?

identify the type of audio

☐ Think about who's speaking.

☐ Think about the information in the audio. Who's it for?

☐ Listen for sounds.

2 a Read the tips in the HOW TO box.

b ▶2.07 Listen to a soundscape and write the type of audio from Exercise 1.

1 _____
2 _____
3 _____
4 _____

3 Which tips in the HOW TO box did you use for help with Exercise 2b? Tick (✓) them.

REACT

4 Work in pairs. Write an announcement and a short conversation for another public place, eg a station or a football stadium.

WORK WITH WORDS Places in public buildings

5 Match the icons (a–j) to the words in the box.

_____ coffee shop	_____ entrance
_____ first floor	_____ gift shop
_____ ground floor	_____ information desk
_____ lift	_____ stairs
_____ ticket office	_____ toilets

6 ▶2.07 Listen to the soundscape again. For each question, choose the correct answer (A, B or C).

1 Where's the coffee shop?
  A in front of the lift
  B next to the gift shop
  C on the first floor

2 The toilets are …
  A on the ground floor.
  B on the first floor.
  C at the top of the stairs.

3 Neil's mother's waiting at …
  A the ticket office.
  B the museum entrance.
  C the information desk.

4 Where does Marta want to go?
  A the gift shop
  B the toilet
  C the coffee shop

7 Work in pairs. Choose a building in your town. Draw a plan of the building and show the position of the different places in Exercise 5. Describe your plan to another pair. Can they identify the place?

This is a plan of …

The entrance is on the ground floor …

GO BEYOND >>

Do the Words & Beyond exercise on page 133.

>>> Workbook, pages 48–49

>>> Talk about how often you do things

READ AND LISTEN >>> Grammar in context

1 ▶2.08 **Read and listen to the radio show. Where's Red Bandana playing today?**

'You're listening to Youth Music Radio on 98.4FM. This week I'm playing a lot of Red Bandana, the all-girl group from Colorado. I love their music. At the moment the group is touring the country and today they're giving a concert at the FIBArk Festival. I'm sure you're all looking forward to it. The girls all live in Colorado. Alexandra plays keyboards, Faith sings and plays bass guitar, Mesa plays drums. Lily usually plays the guitar but sometimes she sings. In fact, she's singing on the song I'm playing now …'

STUDY

2 a <u>Underline</u> **the present continuous verbs in Exercise 1 and circle the present simple verbs.**

b **Complete the explanations. Use Exercise 1 to help you.**

Present continuous and present simple
Use:
Present continuous:
For things in progress now or around now.
Present simple:
For habits, routines and things that are generally true.
Time expressions:
Present continuous: *this week,* _____ , _____ , *now*
Present simple: _____ , _____ , *never, always,* etc

See GRAMMAR DATABASE, page 123.

PRACTISE

3 **Choose the correct words.**

1 It's 6pm on Friday and Amy *goes out* / *'s going out* now.
2 She *usually stays in* / *'s usually staying in* on Fridays.
3 Her cousin Saul *visits* / *'s visiting* from Australia at the moment.
4 In Australia he *lives* / *'s living* in the country.
5 So he *doesn't go out* / *isn't going out* very often.
6 Amy *takes* / *'s taking* him to the city centre.

4 **Write the verbs in the present continuous or present simple.**

(1) _____ (I / like) different types of music. (2) _____ (I / usually / listen to) pop or hip hop but this month (3) _____ (I / listen to) a lot of classical guitar music. (4) _____ (I / learn) the guitar at the moment. (5) _____ (I / go) to classes. In fact, (6) _____ (I / go) to a class right now. Bye!

5 a **Write the music survey questions.**

1 _____ (you / like / music)?
2 Which types of music _____ (you / normally / listen to) – rock, classical, hip hop, pop, reggae … ?
3 What singers or groups _____ (you / listen to) at the moment?
4 _____ (you / learn) a musical instrument right now? If so, which one? If not, which instrument would you like to learn?

b **Write your answers to the questions in Exercise 5a.**

SPEAK

6 **Work in pairs. Ask and answer the questions in the music survey. Then tell the rest of the class about your partner.**

LANGUAGE & BEYOND

13TH BIRTHDAY IDEAS???

VIC245. ▶ **WALL**

Hey! It's my 13th birthday next week and I want to do something REALLY special with about six or seven friends. Mum and Dad say I can choose what to do IF I organise everything. I can spend up to 200 pounds. Any ideas? PLEASE HELP! VIC245.

48 minutes ago · Like

Write a comment…

>>> Find ideas and information

READ AND SPEAK

1 **Work in pairs. Read Vic245's message above and answer the questions.**
   1 Why is she writing the message?
   2 What does she need to do?
   3 What ideas can you give her?

   She can …   *Or maybe she can …*

DO

2 **Work in pairs. Read the answers to Vic245's message. Do they include any of your ideas? Choose the best idea for Vic245's birthday.**

3 **In groups, do the tasks.**
   1 What information does Vic245 need to find for each idea?
   2 Where can she find the information?
   friends   family   TV/radio   the internet   newspapers or magazines

REFLECT

4 **Talk about the questions. Then read the [REFLECTION POINT].**
   1 In what situations do you need to find information?
   2 What ways are there to find information where you live?
   3 What's the best way to find information? Why?

EXTEND

5 **Your class is organising a day trip. You can spend 300–500 euros. In groups, make a list of ideas for things to do. What information do you need and where can you find it? Present two ideas to the rest of the class. Which group has the most popular idea?**

13TH BIRTHDAY IDEAS???

BEST ANSWERS

Is there a theme park near your home? Spend the day there!
GEO3X   48 minutes ago · Like

Go to see a film and then have something to eat near the cinema.
ILOVEFILM   1 hours ago · Like

If you have a video camera, you could make a music video with your friends. What song do you all like?
ASKME88   2 hours ago · Like

Stay in – find a pizza place to order food – watch DVDs – and have a sleepover.
GWARD   5 hours ago · Like

Is anything special happening in your town on your birthday, like a concert or an exhibition?
BB   5 hours ago · Like

PHRASE BYTES

She needs to find out …

She can find the information …

She can ask/look …

REFLECTION POINT

When you organise an event, it's important to think of or find different ideas and then find information about each one. This information can help you make a good decision.

GET THINKING

⫸⫸ Ask for information

SPEAK

1 Work in pairs. Answer the questions.

1 What tourist sights are there in your town or area?
2 What other things can tourists do?
3 Where do tourists get information about sights and events?

WATCH OR LISTEN

2 ▶▶ **2.09 Watch or listen to the scene in the tourist information centre. Are Rose and Luca in the UK? Give reasons for your answer.**

Rose:	Excuse me. Do you speak English?
Assistant:	Yes, I do.
Rose:	Good. Can I ask a question?
Assistant:	Yes, of course.
Rose:	(1) _____ ?
Assistant:	It's on the Museum Island.
Rose:	Thank you.
Assistant:	You're welcome.
Rose:	Sorry, I have another question.
	(2) _____ ?
Assistant:	You can walk. It takes about 10 minutes. Or you can take a bus.
Luca:	Can I ask something else?
Assistant:	Of course.

Luca:	(3) _____ ?
	And (4) _____ ?
Assistant:	Let me check … On Saturdays it opens at 10.00 and closes at 6.00.
Luca:	(5) _____ ?
Assistant:	It costs seven euros. Or you can buy a special ticket to visit all the museums.
Rose:	I don't think we've got time.
Assistant:	(6) _____ ?
Luca:	We're only staying two days.
Assistant:	Well, enjoy your stay!
Rose:	Thank you for your help.
Assistant:	You're welcome.

3 a Complete the questions with the question words in the box.

How	How long	How much	What	When	Where

1 _____ are you staying?
2 _____ 's the Egyptian Museum?
3 _____ does it cost?
4 _____ does it open?
5 _____ time does it close?
6 _____ do we get there?

b ▶ **2.10 Listen and check your answers. Listen again and repeat.**

4 ▶▶ **2.09 Write the questions from Exercise 3a in the conversation. Then watch or listen again and check your answers.**

5 a Read the tips in the HOW TO box.

b Complete the tasks.

1 <u>Underline</u> the polite questions and phrases in the conversation.
2 How does the assistant reply to 'thank you'?

ACT

6 ⊕ **In groups of three, complete the tasks.**

1 Choose a famous city and prepare a scene in a tourist information office. Think of questions to ask about places in the city. Prepare answers to the questions.
2 Act your scene for the class. Can they identify the city?

HOW TO ❓

ask for information

■ Ask if you can ask a question.

■ Use polite phrases: *Excuse me, I'm sorry … .*

■ Thank the other person.

PHRASEBOOK ▶ 2.11 📖

Information questions

Where's the … museum/stadium?

How much does it cost?

When does it open/close?

What time does it open/close?

How do we get there?

Polite questions/phrases and answers

Excuse me. Do you speak English?

Can I ask a question? – Yes, of course.

Sorry, I have another question.

Can I ask something else? – Of course.

Thank you for your help. – You're welcome.

READ

1 Read the notice and find the answers to the questions.

1 Where's the concert?
2 What time does it start?
3 Which bus stops near the concert?
4 What does the price include?
5 How can you find more information?

SCHOOL CONCERT

Come and listen to the school orchestra playing works by
Haydn, Bach and Coldplay!

PLACE
The music room at the Hope Building.

DATES & TIMES
Saturday 7th and Sunday 8th February at 6pm.

HOW TO GET THERE
The number 7 bus stops near the Hope Building.
Parents can park their cars in the main playground.

PRICES
Free for school pupils and children under
14 years old. Adults £3 (price includes tea
and biscuits).

MORE INFORMATION
For more information contact Mrs Henderson.

2 Read the tips in the HOW TO box.

HOW TO
use headings

■ Use a main heading to say what the text is about.
■ Use other headings to help the reader find specific information.

PRACTISE

3 Match the headings (1–5) to the correct information (a–e).

1 Special offer!
2 Contact details
3 Important
4 Opening times
5 Food and drink

a Phone us on 756 200 934.
b Come with two friends and get three tickets for the price of two.
c You can buy drinks and cake at the coffee shop.
d Don't arrive late.
e The library opens at 8.30am and closes at 6.30pm.

PLAN

4 You're going to write a notice for an exhibition at a museum. Use the *Writing plan* to help you prepare.

WRITING PLAN

1 **Choose a museum and think of a theme for the exhibition.**
   What's the exhibition about? What's it called?

2 **Create a notice for the exhibition.**
   What information do you want to include? What pictures can you use?

3 **Use headings to make the information clear.**
   Look at the tips in the HOW TO box.

WRITE AND CHECK

5 Write your notice. Then check it. Tick (✓) the things in the *Writing plan*.

SHARE

6 Swap your notice with other students. Which is the most interesting?

>>> Workbook, pages 52–53

VOCABULARY Activity verbs

1 Write the words with an opposite meaning.

Time Experience

Welcome to the Time Experience at the Science Museum. Travel into the past and in the opposite direction into the future!

1	arrive	l_____
2	come	g_____
3	laugh	c_____
4	open	c_____
5	put on	t_____ o_____
6	get	s_____
7	stand	s_____
8	start	e_____
9	stay in	g_____ o_____
10	talk to	l_____ t_____

___/10

Places in public buildings

2 Complete the Time Experience information with the words in the box.

coffee shop	entrance	first floor
gift shop	ground floor	information desk
lift	stairs	ticket office	toilets

Please buy your tickets at the (1) _____ .
Then walk through the main (2) _____
into the Time Experience.
You can find out about the Time Experience at the
(3) _____ .
Take the fast (4) _____ from the
(5) _____ up to the (6) _____ .
Or walk up the (7) _____ .
At the end of your visit, have a drink in the
(8) _____ .
Buy presents at the (9) _____ .
You can also visit our special Time Experience
(10) _____ for men and women!

___/10

GRAMMAR Present continuous

3 Write the verbs in the present continuous.

1 _____ (you / listen to) the Time Experience audio tour.
2 _____ (you / have) a good time?
3 Right now _____ (we / sit) in the main exhibition room.
4 A special event _____ (happen) here next weekend.
5 Right now, a special video camera _____ (travel) into the future.
6 _____ (we / wait) for the first pictures to arrive.

___/12

Present continuous and present simple

4 Choose the correct words.

INFORMATION

Zach: Where are you? (1) *You always arrive / You're always arriving* on time.
Molly: (2) *We wait / We're waiting* for you on the first floor. (3) *We stand / We're standing* by the information desk.
Zach: Ah! (4) *I know / I'm knowing* where you are. (5) *You don't wait / You aren't waiting* on the first floor. The information desk is on the ground floor!
Molly: Well, in the USA (6) *we always call / we're always calling* this the first floor.
Zach: But (7) *you stay / you're staying* in the UK at the moment and (8) *we call / we're calling* it the ground floor.
Molly: What (9) *do you call / are you calling* the second floor?
Zach: The first floor!

___/18

Your score: ___/50

SKILLS CHECK

✓✓✓	Yes, I can. No problem!
✓✓	Yes, I can. But I need a bit of help.
✓	Yes, I can. But I need a lot of help.

I can understand the order of messages. _____
I can identify the type of audio. _____
I can find ideas and information. _____
I can ask for information in a tourist office. _____
I can use headings. _____

READ

1 **Match the sentences (1–5) to the correct signs and notes (A–H).**

Example:

0 Leave your mobiles at home. *H*

1 This person isn't here now.

2 Don't arrive until the afternoon.

3 Use the other door.

4 There aren't any more tickets for the play.

5 Somebody's got the wrong one.

EXAM TIPS

 match sentences to signs

- Read each sentence first.
- Look for the sign with the same information.
  - Don't always look for the same words.
  - Look for different ways to say the same thing.
- You only need to use five of the signs.

A

RECEPTION
Halwards Hotel
Check-in after 2pm   Check-out before 11am

B

THIS ENTRANCE
IS CLOSED
Please use the entrance on James Street.

C

Return your audio guide to the information desk when you leave.

D

SOLD OUT
There are no more seats for tonight's show.

E

I'm having a coffee at the coffee bar. Back in 30 minutes.

F

PLEASE TAKE OFF YOUR SHOES AT THE FRONT DOOR.

G

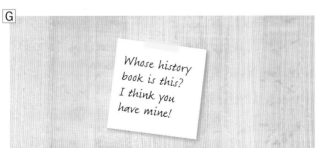

Whose history book is this? I think you have mine!

H

STUDENTS CAN'T TAKE ANY PHONES INTO THE SCHOOL.

Reading: _____ /10

LISTEN

2 ▶2.12 **Listen to the phone conversation and complete the form.**

FREE-TIME ACTIVITIES SURVEY

Age: _13_
Name: (1) _____

STAYING IN
Favourite activity: (2) _____
Type of book/film/game/TV show: (3) _____
Favourite type of music: (4) _____

GOING OUT
Normal weekend activity: (5) _____

Listening: _____ /10

WRITE

3 **Read the note and the information about school uniforms. Then write the information on the shop's order form.**

Mum! School starts next week and I haven't got all of my winter uniform. I can use Ben's old coat and gloves but I need a grey jumper and a scarf. Can you look on the Internet? Don't get the black jumper. The scarf with red stripes isn't for my year, so please get the green one. Thanks. See you later. Ron

GRENVILLE SECONDARY SCHOOL
———— UNIFORM ————

shirt (white) £4.20

scarf (green/red stripes) £4.80

jumper (grey/black) £12.00

trousers (black/grey) £11.00

tie (green/red stripes) £4.20

socks (black/blue) £2.99

ORDER FORM

Name of school: _Grenville Secondary School_
Name of item 1: (1) _____
Colour: (2) _____
Name of item 2: (3) _____
Colour: (4) _____
Total price: (5) _____

Writing: _____ /10

Progress check score _____ /30

EXAM TIPS

 listen and complete notes

- Read the information before you listen.
- Look at the gaps and the words before or after them.
- Decide what type of information you need: times, prices, phone numbers, activities, things, etc.
- Listen for this information and write the numbers or words.
- When you listen again, check your answers.

 listen for specific information
See page 36

EXAM TIPS

 transfer information to a different text

- Read the two texts first. What are they about?
- Now read the task.
  - What information do you need?
  - Where do you think the information is?
- Look for the information in the texts.
- Don't write sentences. Write notes.

 use headings
See page 50

IT'S GOOD FOR YOU!

IN THE PICTURE Food and drink

>>> Talk about food and drink

WORK WITH WORDS Food and drink

1 **RECALL** **Work in pairs. Look at the words and cross out the wrong word in each group. Can you say why it's different? You have one minute.**

1 mineral water, ~~fish~~, juice, coffee
The other words are drinks.
2 banana, egg, apple, orange
3 pizza, salad, bread, sandwich
4 milk, rice, cheese, ice cream
5 steak, pasta, burger, chicken

2 a **Work in pairs. Look at the photos (a–l) in Dan's blog and complete the list (1–12) of food and drinks. Use the words in the box.**

butter	cake	carrot	chips	chocolate	cola	onion
potato	soup	sweets	tomato	yoghurt		

b ▶2.13 **Dan is showing his blog to his new friend Myra. Listen and complete or check your answers from Exercise 2a.**

c ▶2.14 **Listen and repeat the food and drink words.**

3 a ▶2.15 **PRONOUNCE** **Listen to the words.**

1 How many syllables are there?
2 <u>Underline</u> the stress. Which words have the same stress?

potato   tomato   banana   fantastic   vegetable   seventeen

b ▶2.16 **Listen again and repeat.**

4 **Look at the words in Exercise 2a. Find …**

1 something red
2 two vegetables
3 something with egg in it
4 two white foods
5 a drink
6 something you put on bread
7 something you can eat and drink
8 something children (and some adults!) like

5 🗣 **Work in pairs. Describe what the boy is doing and eating in each picture. Are the food and activities healthy or unhealthy?**

6 **THE MOVING PICTURE** ▶ **Watch the video. What food do you see?**

1
2
3
4
5
6
7
8
9
10
11
12

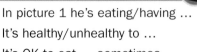

PHRASE BYTES

In picture 1 he's eating/having …

It's healthy/unhealthy to …

It's OK to eat … sometimes, but …

SPEAK

7 a Work in pairs. Do the survey. Ask your partner the questions and write his/her answers.

😊 HEALTHY AND HAPPY SURVEY

1 How do you get to school?
   A I walk or cycle.
   B I take the bus.
   C My parents take me in the car.

2 How much sport do you do?
   A lots
   B a bit
   C no sport

3 How often do you eat chips and sweets?
   A not very often
   B sometimes
   C most days

Back   Next

b Check your partner's answers on page 142. Read out what the survey says. Does your partner agree?

GO BEYOND

Do the Words & Beyond exercise on page 134.

READING What's for lunch?

>>> Identify who a text is for

SPEAK AND READ

1 a Work in pairs. Look at the photos of school lunch in different countries. Describe what you can see in each photo.

   b Which lunch would you like to eat? Why?

2 a Read the tips in the **HOW TO** box.

   b **▶2.17** Read the text and identify who the text is for.

   A parents   B students   C teachers   D school cooks

 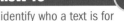
HOW TO ?

identify who a text is for

☐ Identify the type of text (see page 12).

☐ Read the first few lines and underline important words.

☐ Decide who the readers are (teenagers/adults/experts).

PARK SCHOOL BLOG

School lunch around the world   BLOG ABOUT CONTACT

Our class is doing a project about school lunches around the world. Read other students' descriptions and add a description of your school lunch. Don't forget to send a photo!

Mikkel, Denmark
All students here take a packed lunch to school. I usually have brown bread with cheese and salad and an apple. We can't take any unhealthy food like chocolate, sweets or fizzy drinks.

Jalissa, USA
We eat things like taco salad, pizza or burgers. We always get milk or juice and some vegetables or fruit.

Dae-Ho, Korea
I like the food at my school but we don't get many different things. We usually get soup, some vegetables with rice and a lot of salad. We don't get much meat.

Mathilde, France
We have salad or a vegetable dish, and then meat with sauce and potatoes or fish with lemon. My favourite is mussels with chips. Then we have yoghurt or some cheese, and after that we have dessert.

Camila, Ecuador
There isn't any lunch at my school, so I have lunch at home with my family after school. We usually eat soup and then rice with vegetables and chicken or fish.

---

3 Which tips in the **HOW TO** box did you use for help with Exercise 2b? Tick (✓) them.

4 Read the descriptions again. Which lunches have no meat or not much meat? Which lunch has dessert?

REACT

5 Work in pairs. Tell your partner about your school lunch. Then describe your dream lunch.

GO BEYOND >>>

Write a school lunch menu for two days.

>>> Describe how much there is of something

READ AND LISTEN >>> Grammar in context

1 **(►2.18) Read and listen to the conversation. What's for dinner?**

Danny: Hi Mum. I'm hungry! What's for dinner?
Mum: I don't know – we haven't got much food.
Danny: I'd like eggs with some chips.
Mum: Yes, I'd like that too. But we haven't got any eggs – or any potatoes. There aren't many other things. We've got some tomatoes and a lot of salad.
Danny: How many tomatoes have we got? Have we got any pasta?
Mum: Yes, there are a lot of tomatoes and there's some spaghetti.
Danny: What about some spaghetti with tomato sauce and some salad? I can cook!

STUDY

2 **Complete the explanations with the correct words from Exercise 1.**

Countable and uncountable nouns

Use and form:
Countable nouns (*an egg*, *a chip*, *a* _____ ,
a _____) have a singular and a plural form.
Uncountable nouns (*food*, *salad*, _____ ,
_____) don't have a plural form.
See GRAMMAR DATABASE, page 124.

3 **Complete the diagram with *a lot of, not much, not many* and *some*.**

0 ——————————————————— +++
not any _____ _____ _____

4 **Complete the explanations with *countable* and *uncountable*. Use exercises 1 and 2 to help you.**

A lot of, much, many, some and any

Form and use:
a lot of (countable and uncountable): all sentences
much (_____) and *many* (_____):
negative sentences, questions
We haven't got much food.
How many tomatoes have we got?

any (countable and uncountable): negative sentences, most questions
Have we got any pasta?

some (countable and uncountable): positive sentences, questions with offers and requests
What about some spaghetti?
See GRAMMAR DATABASE, page 124.

PRACTISE

5 **Look at the café menu. Choose the correct options.**

Café Beyond

Food
Sandwiches: cheese, egg, salad, steak, chicken, chicken curry
Pizza: cheese and tomato
Pasta: cheese sauce, vegetable sauce
Steak: with chips or salad
Cake: chocolate, apple

Drinks
Mineral water, orange juice, grape juice, banana juice, cola
Tea, coffee, hot chocolate

1 A There aren't any sandwiches.
  B There are a lot of sandwiches.
2 A There isn't any pasta.
  B There's some pasta but not much.
3 A There are a lot of drinks.
  B There aren't many drinks.
4 A There isn't much meat.
  B There isn't any meat.
5 A There are some pizzas on the menu.
  B There's a pizza on the menu.

6 **Complete the conversation with *a(n), some, any, a lot of, much* or *many*.**

Mum: I want (1) _____ pizza. But there aren't (2) _____ different pizzas. So I'd like (3) _____ pasta with cheese sauce. But I don't want (4) _____ sauce, just a little.
Danny: I'd like (5) _____ steak but I don't want (6) _____ salad at all. I want (7) _____ chips – (8) _____ chips; I'm really hungry. Is there (9) _____ apple juice?
Mum: No, there isn't. What about (10) _____ banana juice?
Danny: Banana juice?!!

SPEAK

7 **Work in pairs. Look at the menu in Exercise 5. Talk about what you want / don't want to eat.**

I want a chicken curry sandwich.

There isn't any salad, so I'd like a salad sandwich.

I don't want any chips.

There aren't many types of cake.

I'd like some chocolate cake.

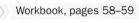

SPEAK AND LISTEN

1 Do a class survey about how many hours you sleep.

- One person asks: *Who sleeps for six hours? Who sleeps for seven hours?*, etc.
- Put up your hand.
- One person writes the results on the board: *six hours: five people …*

2 a Read the tips in the HOW TO box.

b ▶2.19 Listen to four speakers in a radio report about sleep. Who are they?

I think Speaker 1 is a teacher …

3 Which tips in the HOW TO box did you use for help with Exercise 2b? Tick (✓) them.

4 ▶2.19 Listen again. There's one question for each speaker. Choose A, B or C.

1 How do the students look in class?

 A   B   C

2 What time does the speaker get up?

 A   B   C

3 How do teens feel when they don't sleep enough?

 A   B   C

4 How many hours of sleep does a teenager need?

 A   B   C

| HOW TO |
| identify the speaker |
| ☐ Listen to the voice. Is the speaker young or old? |
| ☐ Listen for the general topic. |
| ☐ Listen carefully for the names of people and places. |

REACT

5 Work in pairs. Answer the questions.

1 Do you sleep enough? 2 Look at your class sleep times on the board. Does everybody sleep enough?

WORK WITH WORDS Lifestyle adjectives

6 a ▶2.20 Match the words (a–j) to the quotes (1–10). Then listen and check.

1 'I have a lot of energy and interests. a tired
2 'My body's healthy and I do a lot of exercise.' b lucky
3 'I need to sleep now.' c busy
4 'I have a lot of things to do.' d active
5 'Good things always happen to me.' e fit
6 'I don't feel happy.' f ill
7 'I feel bad because I have a lot of things to do.' g lazy
8 'I feel good.' h stressed
9 'I have a health problem.' i unhappy
10 'I never want to do anything.' j well

b ▶2.21 Listen again and repeat.

7 Work in pairs. Answer the questions.

1 Do you feel fit and well?
2 Are you tired now? Why?
3 Are you stressed? Why?

GO BEYOND ▶▶

Do the Words & Beyond exercise on page 134.

1 Read Marc's likes and dislikes. Do you like and dislike these things?

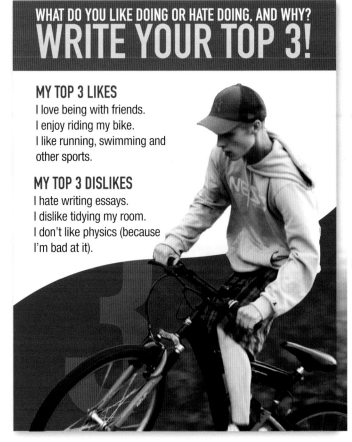

WHAT DO YOU LIKE DOING OR HATE DOING, AND WHY?

WRITE YOUR TOP 3!

MY TOP 3 LIKES
I love being with friends.
I enjoy riding my bike.
I like running, swimming and other sports.

MY TOP 3 DISLIKES
I hate writing essays.
I dislike tidying my room.
I don't like physics (because I'm bad at it).

STUDY

2 Complete the explanations with the correct words from Exercise 1.

Like + -ing

Use: To talk about your likes and dislikes.

Likes: *like,* _____ 👍
and _____ 👍👍
Dislikes: *don't like,* _____ 👎
and _____ 👎👎

Form:
With a noun: *I don't like **physics**.*
With a verb + *-ing*: *I like **running**.*
See GRAMMAR DATABASE, page 124.

3 Write the correct spelling of the *-ing* form. Look at Exercise 1.

1 be _____   4 write _____
2 tidy _____   5 run _____
3 ride _____   6 swim _____

PRACTISE

4 a Complete Susie13's reply on the forum. Use the *-ing* form of the verbs.

MY TOP 3 LIKES
I enjoy (1) _____ (play) online video games with my friends.
I like (2) _____ (travel) and
(3) _____ (visit) new places.
I love (4) _____ (dance) and other activities.

MY TOP 3 DISLIKES
I don't like (5) _____ (get) up early.
I hate (6) _____ (wait) for things.
I don't like (7) _____ (keep) my room tidy
or (8) _____ (make) my bed.

b What do Susie13 and Marc both like? What do they both dislike?

5 Complete the sentences with your top three likes and dislikes.

👍

1 I like _____ .
2 I enjoy _____ .
3 I love _____ .

👎

4 I don't like _____ .
5 I dislike _____ .
6 I hate _____ .

6 a Write the questions.

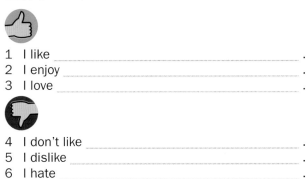

1 you / like / go / to school?
   Do you like going to school?
2 you / enjoy / speak / English?
3 you / like / use social networking sites?
4 you enjoy / meet / new people?
5 you / like / cook?
6 you / like / shop for clothes?

b Write one more question for a partner.

SPEAK

7 Work in pairs. Ask your partner a question from Exercise 6. Then ask *Why?* or *Why not?*

Do you like going to school?   *Yes, I do.*

Why?   *I see my friends there.*

LANGUAGE BEYOND

>>> **Follow the rules in electronic communication**

SPEAK AND READ

1 **Work in pairs. How often do you do the things below? Tell a partner.**

- Send text messages on my phone.
- Write instant messages (IMs) to my friends on the internet.
- Send emails.
- Write comments on an internet forum.
- Write comments on social networking sites.

2 ◯ **Read the situations (1–3). How do you feel if they happen to you? Tell a partner.**

DO

3 **Match four rules to the situations in Exercise 2. Which one is a good rule for all the situations?**

a Everything you write on the internet stays on the internet. ....
b Can't say it face-to-face? Don't write it. ....
c Ask before you share information or photos of other people. ....
d Don't write things when you're tired or stressed. ....
e Think before you send a message or put something on the internet. ....

REFLECT

4 **Talk about the questions. Then read the** **REFLECTION POINT** **.**

1 You want to say something important to a friend. Is it a good idea to say it …
   face-to-face / by phone / by text message / on the internet? Why?
2 How often do you or your friends have problems like the situations in Exercise 2?
3 What can you do if others send you hate messages?

EXTEND

5 **Work in small groups. Write two or three more rules for electronic communication.**

RESPECT OTHERS

How do you feel?

1 You get a text message on your phone from a friend. It starts *'Hi Jo, Jem is so lazy! I hate lazy people! …'* But Jem is your name – Jo is another friend. You get the message by mistake.

2 You write a silly personal story on your blog late at night. The next day you delete it. But it's still on the internet when you search.

3 You put a funny photo of a friend on your social networking page. The next day your friend phones – and your friend doesn't think it's funny.

PHRASE BYTES

I feel angry/sad/stupid …

I feel bad/sorry because I …

I think it's rude / a bad idea to …

REFLECTION POINT

Be polite on the internet and in text messages. Think before you send a message or put something on the internet. Remember: always tell the website or your parents about hate messages or problems.

>>> React to news

SPEAK

1 **Work in pairs. Look at the photos. Who do you think is giving ...**
  - good and bad news?
  - bad news?
  - surprising news?

WATCH OR LISTEN

2 ▶▶ **2.22** **Watch or listen to the scenes. Check your answer from Exercise 1. What's the news?**

2
Luca: My grandma's in hospital. She's really ill.
May: I'm (3) _____ , Luca. That's so (4) _____ .

1
Adam: No more chips from fast-food places for me!
Rose: Really? I don't (1) _____ it.
Adam: Do you know, they put sugar on chips?
Rose: That's (2) _____ .

3
Liz: Guess what? Tomorrow we have two extra PE lessons. No maths test!
Skye: Wow! Great! ... That's (5) _____ !
Liz: It's a 10-kilometre run.
Skye: Oh. That's (6) _____ ! ... I want to do the maths test.

3 a ▶▶ **2.22** **Watch or listen again. Complete the conversations with the words in the box.**

| amazing | believe | fantastic | sad | sorry | terrible |

b ▶ **2.23** **Listen to the phrases and check.**

4 ▶ **2.24** **Listen and repeat all the phrases in the** PHRASEBOOK **.**

ACT

5 a 🔊 **Work in pairs and take it in turns. Practise reacting to news.**
  - Choose four of the situations in the box.
  - Give the news to your partner.
  - Your partner reacts.

> You're moving to a different town.
> You have a new baby brother.
> You don't want to eat sweets anymore.
> You're in a new TV programme.
> Your school is closing.
> You feel tired and stressed.

b **Think of two new situations. Give your partner the news. React to your partner's news.**

PHRASEBOOK ▶ **2.25**

React to good news
Great!
That's fantastic!
Wow!
React to bad news
I'm sorry.
That's so sad.
That's terrible.
React to surprising news
Really?
I don't believe it!
That's amazing!

>>> Use *because*

SPEAK AND READ

1 Work in pairs. Tell your partner your favourite food and drinks. Do you like the same things?

2 Read the comment on the *Ask Anything* site. What's Alejandro's favourite meal, dessert and drink?

What's your favourite meal?

My favourite meal is tacos with meat, onions, some lettuce, tomatoes and a lot of cheese. I love tacos because my mum makes them at home. They're fantastic. I like helping her (but I hate cleaning the kitchen after!). My favourite dessert is chocolate ice cream with a lot of chocolate sauce. I always drink water with meals because fizzy drinks are really bad for your teeth and I don't like them.
Alejandro

[new post] [reply]

✔ Get it right

Use -s for the plural of most nouns with -o (eg *tacos*).

Learn nouns with the plural -oes (eg *tomatoes, potatoes*).

3 a Read the tips in the **HOW TO** box.

HOW TO ❓

use *because*

- Use *because* to give reasons and answer the question *Why?*
- Use *because* + name (*I, she*, etc) + verb.
- Don't use a comma before *because*.

b **Find the answers to these questions in Alejandro's comment.**
1 Why do you like tacos?
2 Why do you drink water with meals?

PRACTISE

4 **Match to make sentences.**
1 I don't like grapes because
2 I love vegetables because
3 I don't eat steak because
4 I drink milk before bed because
5 I love chocolate because

a I never eat meat.
b I feel happy when I eat it.
c it makes me sleep.
d they're good for you.
e I hate all fruit.

PLAN

5 **You're going to write a description of your favourite meal. Use the *Writing plan* to help you prepare.**

WRITING PLAN

1 **Say what your favourite meal is.**
What's in it? How often do you eat it? Why do you like eating it? (use *because*)

2 **Say what your favourite dessert is.**
What do you eat with it (eg ice cream, chocolate sauce)? Is it only for special days? When do you usually eat it?

3 **Say what your favourite drink is.**
What is it? Do you drink it every day? Why do you like it? (use *because*)

WRITE AND CHECK

6 **Write your description. Then check it. Tick (✓) the things in the plan.**

SHARE

7 **Swap your description with other students. Read their descriptions. Which meals would you like to eat?**

UNIT REVIEW

5

VOCABULARY Food and drink

1 Label the food (1–12) with the words in the box.

butter   cake   carrots   chips
chocolate   cola   onion   potatoes
soup   sweets   tomatoes   yoghurt

SCHOOL SUPERMARKET DAY

Buy food on School Supermarket Day from our website.
Your family gets good food – and we give your school some of the
money to buy books and other things.

1 ___   2 ___   3 ___   4 ___   5 ___   6 ___

7 ___   8 ___   9 ___   10 ___   11 ___   12 ___

___ /12

Lifestyle adjectives

2 Complete the adjectives.

Do you have a (1) b_____y and
(2) a_____e life? Do you feel
(3) t_____d, (4) s_____d,
(5) u_____y or (6) i___l?
Too (7) l_____y to go shopping for healthy food? It's
your (8) l_____y day – it's School Supermarket
day! Shop online now! Eat our healthy food and feel
(9) f___t and (10) w_____l in no time!

___ /10

GRAMMAR A lot of, much, many, some and any

3 Choose the correct words.

Our meals don't cost (1) *many / much* money and you don't need
(2) *some / any* special ideas.
Our tip: buy (3) *a lot of / much*
vegetables and (4) *a / some* rice.
You don't need (5) *many / much*
minutes to make (6) *a / some*
healthy meal. Do you have (7) *a / any* questions? We have (8) *a lot of / any* other tips for you. See our
FAQ page!

___ /16

Like + -ing

4 Complete the sentences with *like, enjoy, love, don't like, dislike,* and *hate*. (Sometimes two words are possible.) Use the correct -ing form.

WHAT OTHER SUPERMARKET DAY STUDENTS SAY:

My parents (1) _____ (👍 / help) the school. I
(2) _____ (👍 / eat) the food!

Usually I (3) _____ (👎 / try) different things. But I
(4) _____ (👍 / choose) Supermarket Day food.

I (5) _____ (👎👎 / shop)
in the supermarket with Dad. But
we (6) _____ (👍👍 / buy)
Supermarket Day food online.

___ /12

Your score: ___ /50

SKILLS CHECK

✓✓✓	Yes, I can. No problem!
✓✓	Yes, I can. But I need a bit of help.
✓	Yes, I can. But I need a lot of help.

I can identify who a text is for. _____
I can identify the speaker. _____
I can follow the rules in electronic communication. _____
I can react to news. _____
I can use *because* when I write. _____

UNIT 6 IT'S YOUR TURN

IN THE PICTURE In the game

>>> Talk about sports and games

WORK WITH WORDS Sports and games

1 **RECALL** Work in pairs. Complete the sports. You have two minutes.

-ball: bas _k e t b a l l_ , bas _____ ,
vol _____ , fo _____
-ing: sw _____ , hor _____ -ri _____ ,
sur _____ , sai _____ , sk _____ ,
cy _____ , i _____ sk _____
Other: go _l f_ , te _____ , ho _____ ,
tab _____ te _____

2 Work in pairs. Try and match the photos to some of the sports and games in the box. Then look on page 142 to check your answers.

___ badminton	___ bowling	___ chess
___ gymnastics	___ ice hockey	___ rugby

3 ▶2.26 Listen and match the sounds (1–6) to the sports and games in the box.

___ American football	___ cards	___ cricket
___ skateboarding	___ snowboarding	___ video games

4 a Copy and complete the table with the sports and games in exercises 2 and 3.

play (games, ball sports)	go (-ing sports)	do (other)
cards		

b ▶2.27 Listen and check your answers. Then listen and repeat the expressions.

5 **THE MOVING PICTURE** ▶ Watch the video and guess the sports and games.

1
5
6

6 **Work in pairs. Answer the questions in the quiz.**

7 **You can add *-er* to some sports and verbs to describe the player. You can't add *-er* to two words below. Which words? What's the player called?**

Sports: football, golf, gymnastics, cricket
Verbs: run, swim, cycle, surf, skateboard

SPEAK

8 a **Complete the sentences with sports, games and people.**

I like playing/going/doing …
I love watching …
I don't like …
I hate watching …
My favourite [sports player] is …
My favourite team is …

b 🔄 **Work in pairs. Ask questions to compare your sentences.**

GAME ON! ♟

How many questions in our sports and games quiz can you answer correctly?

1 It's similar to rugby. It's the number one sport in one country but it isn't very popular in other countries.
   A baseball   **B** ice hockey   **C** American football

2 This is a very old game. When you play with friends, it's a game. In big competitions, it's a sport.
   A cards   **B** chess   **C** bowling

3 It's the world's number two sport because it's popular in two big countries – India and Pakistan.
   A cricket   **B** football   **C** basketball

4 Over 100 million people do board sports around the world. What's the original board sport?
   A surfing   **B** snowboarding   **C** skateboarding

5 China is the number one country in the world in some popular sports. Which one(s)?
   A gymnastics   **B** badminton   **C** table tennis

PHRASE BYTES

Do you like playing/going/watching … ?

What's/Who's your favourite … ?

GO BEYOND

Do the Words & Beyond exercise on page 135.

⟫⟫⟫ Workbook, page 68

SPEAK AND READ

1 **Work in pairs. Answer the questions about your country.**

1 Make a list of famous sportsmen and women. What sports do they play?
2 Who are the sports stars of the future?

2 a **Look at the title of the text and the photos. What do you think it's about?**

b ▶2.28 **Read the text and check your answer.**

3 a **Read the tips in the** **HOW TO** **box.**

PROGRAMME GUIDE

THE NEXT BIG THING: THE FINAL

Channel 7, Saturday, 7pm

HOW TO

understand new words (1)

☐ Identify the type of word. Is it a verb, noun or adjective?

☐ Do you know a similar word? Does it help you understand the new word?

THE SHOW

The final is here. There are just two **competitors** now: hockey player Judy Cole and tennis player Mahesh Nayar. Only one can be our next big thing and one of the future **superstars** of their sport.
They're both strong and fast. They're both **competitive**. But **viewers** of this programme know that sports stars need other **abilities** too. Can they think quickly? Can they play well in a team? Do they **train** hard? To find out, watch the final this Saturday.

THE COMPETITORS

Judy's only 13 but she plays in her city's under-15 team. She can't run very fast, but she can think quickly and she always makes good decisions – and she can get better. At the moment she doesn't always communicate well with other players on her team and she gets stressed easily in difficult matches. But she's working hard on these things.

Mahesh has a natural talent. He can serve fast and he moves very well when he's playing. But his game goes up and down. He usually plays brilliantly, but there are days when he can't concentrate and he plays badly. The problem is, he can't practise every day. He also wants to be a doctor, so he studies a lot too.

b **Look at the words in bold in the text. What do you think they mean? Use the tips in the** **HOW TO** **box to help you.**

c **Match the words in bold to the definitions (1–6) to check your answers.**

1 things that you can do
2 always trying to be the winner
3 people watching a TV programme
4 practise an activity
5 people in a competition
6 very famous people

4 **Which tips in the** **HOW TO** **box did you use for help with Exercise 3b? Tick (✓) them.**

5 **Work in pairs. Read about the competitors.**
Student A: Read about Judy. Student B: Read about Mahesh. Then tell your partner about your competitor.

REACT

6 **Work in pairs. Answer the questions.**

1 Which competitor is the next big thing? Give your opinion and explain why.
2 Would you like to watch the programme? Why?/Why not?

GO BEYOND

Don't look at the descriptions. Make a list of what the competitors can do. Then read the descriptions again to check.

GRAMMAR *Can/can't* for ability; adverbs of manner

>>> Talk about what you can do and how you do it

READ AND LISTEN >>> Grammar in context

1 ▶ 2.29 **Read and listen to the interview. When does the school badminton club train?**

Kim: So, you want to join the school badminton club. Can you play badminton?

Sophie: Yes, I can. I can't play very **well** but I learn **quickly**.

Kim: Can you get up **early**? We train at 7am.

Sophie: I can be here for 7.

Kim: Can you stay **late** on Wednesdays? We sometimes have matches.

Sophie: No, I can't. I've got a piano lesson and I can't change it very **easily**.

STUDY

2 **Complete the explanations with the correct words from Exercise 1.**

Can/can't for ability

Use: For things you have the ability or time to do.

Form:

Positive and negative
I/you/he, etc + *can/can't* + verb
I _____ here for 7.
I _____ very well.

Questions and short answers
Can + *I/you/she*, etc + verb
_____ badminton?
Yes, I can. / No, she can't.

See GRAMMAR DATABASE, page 125.

3 **Complete with examples from Exercise 1.**

Adverbs of manner

Use: To say how you do something

Form:
adjective + *-ly*
quick > _____ ,
easy > _____
(Spelling rules: Page 125)

Irregular adverbs:
hard, fast, _____ and *late* are adjectives <u>and</u> adverbs.
good > _____

Word order:
She **trains hard.**
She can't change **her lesson** *very easily.*
See GRAMMAR DATABASE, page 125.

PRACTISE

4 ▶ 2.30 **Complete the conversation. Use *can/can't*, the verbs in brackets and short answers. Then listen and check.**

Kim: What do you think of Sophie?

Mia: She (1) *can play* (play ✓) quite well. But she's got some bad habits and she (2) _____ (change ✗) them.

Kim: (3) _____ (she / get) to training on time?

Mia: Yes, she (4) _____ . She's always on time. But she (5) _____ (come ✗) on Wednesdays.

Kim: So (6) _____ (she / play) in competitions for the club?

Mia: No, she (7) _____ . She (8) _____ (train ✓) with us but she needs to get better first.

5 **Complete the advert with the adverb form of the words.**

Greenmore School's Annual Talent Show

Can you do maths (1) _____ (fast)? Can you sing (2) _____ (good)? Can you play the piano (3) _____ (perfect)? Can you remember things (4) _____ (easy)? If you've got a talent, enter our talent show before the end of this month. But do it (5) _____ (quick). You can't be in the show if your entry arrives (6) _____ (late).

6 **Write the sentences with adverbs.**

Silvia Williams, karate
1 She obviously trains. (hard) _____

2 She moves. (slow) _____

Seamus and Mary Begley
3 They can sing. (beautiful) _____
4 He plays the guitar. (bad) _____

Ivan Perez, comedian
5 He speaks in public. (confident) _____
6 He can't tell jokes. (good) _____

WRITE AND SPEAK

7 a **Write four questions for a partner to discover his/her talents. Use exercises 5 and 6 to help you.**

Can you run fast?
Yes, I can.

Can you tell jokes well?
No, I can't, but I can …

b **Work in pairs. Ask your questions. Then tell the class about your partner's talents.**

LISTENING AND VOCABULARY Game over

>>> **Understand spoken instructions**

SPEAK AND LISTEN

1 **Work in pairs. Talk about video games.**
- What are your favourite games? Where do you play them – on a phone, tablet, console, … ?
- If you don't play video games, what do you do in your free time?

2 a **Read the tips in the (HOW TO) box.**

b ▶2.31 **Listen to Jan and Gavin talking about three different games. For each game, put the screens in the correct order.**

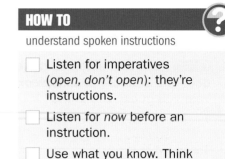

HOW TO

understand spoken instructions

☐ Listen for imperatives (*open, don't open*): they're instructions.

☐ Listen for *now* before an instruction.

☐ Use what you know. Think about the next instruction.

3 **Which tips in the (HOW TO) box did you use for help with Exercise 2b? Tick (✓) them.**

4 ▶2.31 **Listen again and complete the information about the games.**

Game 1: At the start the fox tries to _____ the chicken.
The chicken goes into a _____ so the fox can't see it.
Game 2: Jan chooses a _____ at the start.
During the game you go up a _____ .
Game 3: It's a very _____ game.
Gavin can't _____ the aliens.

REACT

5 **Work in pairs. Which of the three games would you like to play? Tell your partner.**

WORK WITH WORDS Games verbs

6 a **Match the screens (a–i) in Exercise 2b to the games verbs in the box. You need to match two verbs to screen g.**

___ climb	___ destroy	___ hit	___ jump	___ look for
___ lose	___ move	___ shoot	___ throw	___ win

b ▶2.32 **Listen and check. Then listen and repeat the verbs.**

7 a ▶2.33 (PRONOUNCE) **The vowel in *lose*, *move* and *shoot* has an /uː/ sound. Listen and repeat the verbs.**

b ▶2.34 **Listen and write six other words with the /uː/ sound. Then listen and repeat the words.**

8 **Work in pairs. Complete task A or B.**
- **A** Describe a video game but don't say its name. Can your partner guess the game?
- **B** Invent a new video game. Then describe it to other students.

GO BEYOND >>

Do the Words & Beyond exercise on page 135.

READ AND LISTEN >>> Grammar in context

1 ▶2.35 **Read and listen to the conversation. Find the board, dice and pieces in the photo. Can you guess the game?**

Sima: Let's play my favourite game.
Tony: What is it?
Sima: You have to guess.
Tony: OK. Is it a board game?
Sima: Yes, it is.
Tony: Do players have to use dice?
Sima: Yes, they do. Then you move your piece to the right square. If it's a street, you can buy it. You don't have to buy it but it's a good idea.
Tony: That's easy! It's …

STUDY

2 **Complete the explanations with examples from Exercise 1.**

Have to and *don't have to*

Use:
have to: when something is necessary
don't have to: when something isn't necessary

Form:
Positive and negative
I/he, etc + *have/has to* + verb

_____

I/he, etc + *don't/doesn't have to* + verb

_____

Questions and short answers
Do/Does + *I/she*, etc + *have to* + verb

_____

Yes, I do. / Yes, she does.
No, I don't. / No, she doesn't.
See GRAMMAR DATABASE, page 125.

PRACTISE

3 ▶2.36 **Complete the conversation with *have to* and short answers. Then listen and check. What's the game?**

Tony: Let's play my favourite game now. In this game each player (1) *has to move* (move) pieces around a board too.
Sima: (2) _____ (you / play) on a special board?
Tony: Yes, you (3) _____ .
Sima: Is it a difficult game? (4) _____ (players / think) a lot?
Tony: No, they (5) _____ . It's not chess! You (6) _____ (not learn) a lot of rules.
Sima: What (7) _____ (a player / do) to win?
Tony: He or she (8) _____ (take) all the other player's pieces.

4 **Choose the correct words.**

You (1) *have to / don't have to* play golf with another person. You can play alone.

In rugby a player (2) *has to / doesn't have to* throw the ball to another player behind him. You can't throw it to a player in front of you.

Bowling's great because you (3) *have to / don't have to* buy any equipment. They give it to you when you play. Also it (4) *has to / doesn't have to* be a competitive game. You can play just for fun.

In chess the player with the white pieces (5) *has to / doesn't have to* move first. In some competitions they play with a clock. If you're playing with friends you (6) *have to / don't have to* do that.

5 **Complete the description with *have to* and *don't have to* and the verbs in the box. What's the sport?**

have	hit	learn	~~play~~	wear

1 You can't play alone. You *have to play* with one or three other people.
2 You _____ any special clothes but it's a good idea to wear trainers.
3 You _____ the right equipment to play the game. You can't play without it.
4 It's a simple game. You _____ any difficult rules.
5 You _____ the ball to the other player or players. They try to hit it back.

The sport is: _____

WRITE AND SPEAK

6 a **Write three or four sentences about a game or sport using *have to* and *don't have to*.**

b **Work in pairs. Read your sentences to your partner. Try to guess your partner's game or sport. Ask questions with *Do you have to … ?* if you need other clues.**

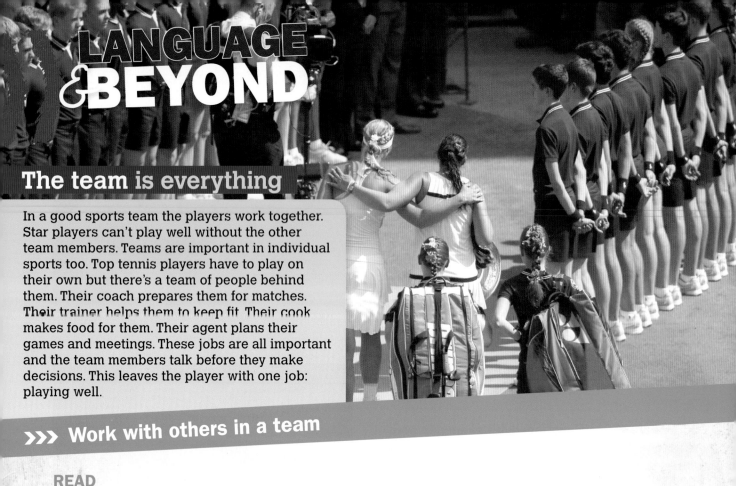

LANGUAGE &BEYOND

The team is everything

In a good sports team the players work together. Star players can't play well without the other team members. Teams are important in individual sports too. Top tennis players have to play on their own but there's a team of people behind them. Their coach prepares them for matches. Their trainer helps them to keep fit. Their cook makes food for them. Their agent plans their games and meetings. These jobs are all important and the team members talk before they make decisions. This leaves the player with one job: playing well.

>>> Work with others in a team

READ

1 Read the article above. Who's in a tennis player's team?

DO

2 Work in groups. Choose the correct words about a good team. Use Exercise 1 to help you.

1 Team members *do / don't do* different jobs.
2 *All / Not all* team members have an important job to do.
3 They *don't listen / listen* to the opinions of the other team members.
4 They *make / don't make* decisions together.

3 ◯ In your group, follow the instructions and make a sports team.

1 Find out about your team members' skills in different sports.
2 Choose one team member to be the team's star player.
3 Talk about possible jobs for other team members, eg be the trainer, cook, agent or official photographer, start a fan club … .
4 Choose a job for every member of the team.

4 Make a plan for the next three days. Decide what each team member has to do. Then tell other teams about your plan.

REFLECT

5 Talk about the questions. Then read the (REFLECTION POINT).

1 What good sports teams do you know? Why are they good?
2 Think about Exercise 3. Is it easy to make a team? Why?/Why not?
3 What are the good and bad things about working in a team?

EXTEND

6 Work in teams. You're organising a show to make money for a children's hospital. Choose a job for everyone and make a plan.

Possible jobs: perform (Can you sing, dance, play an instrument or tell jokes?), make posters, prepare food to sell, talk to TV and radio stations …

> **PHRASE BYTES**
>
> What sports can you do well, … ?
> I can swim/play …
> Somebody can be/start/make …
> I think the team needs a/some …
> Who can … ?
> I can … . I love …

> **REFLECTION POINT**
>
> In good teams every member has a job that they can do well. Team members also make decisions together. Sometimes there's a leader but they can't do their job well without the team.

COMMUNICATE & COOPERATE

>>> Workbook, page 77

>>> Ask for and give or refuse permission

SPEAK

1 **Work in groups. Make a list of things you need permission to do. Who do you ask for permission?**

WATCH OR LISTEN

2 **2.37 Watch or listen to the scenes. What do Alex, Amy and Joe ask to do?**

1

Alex: (1) _____ use the laptop for my homework?
Mum: Of course you can.
Alex: (2) _____ if I take it to Sam's house tomorrow?
Mum: I'm sorry, but I need it. I've got some work.

2

Amy: (3) _____ if I finish training early today?
Teacher: (4) _____ ask why?
Amy: I have to go to the dentist's.
Teacher: All right.

3

Joe: (5) _____ if I play a video game?
Dad: Yes, but you have to tidy your room first.
Joe: OK. (6) _____ go skateboarding this afternoon?
Dad: No, you can't. We've got other plans.

---

3 **2.37 Complete each conversation with two questions. Then watch or listen again and check or complete your answers.**

4 <u>Underline</u> **the answers to the questions in the conversations.**

5 **2.38 Listen and repeat the questions and answers.**

ACT

6 **Work in pairs. Prepare a conversation for each situation. Then present your conversations to other students.**

1 **You:** Ask for permission to stay at a friend's house on Saturday.
Your parent: Give permission, but only if he/she does all his/her homework first.
2 **You:** Ask for permission to go home early because you don't feel well.
Your teacher: Refuse permission, but say he/she can go and see the nurse.

PHRASE BYTES

I need permission to use/watch/go to …

I ask … for permission to …

I need my …'s permission to …

PHRASEBOOK 2.39

Ask for permission

Can I/we … ?

Is it OK / all right if I/we … ?

Give or refuse permission

✓ Yes, you can.

Of course.

All right / OK.

Yes, but only if …

✗ No, you can't.

I'm sorry, but …

SPEAK AND READ

1 Work in pairs. Answer the questions.

  1 Who are your sporting heroes?
  2 Why do you admire them?

2 Read the profile. Why does Anna admire her sporting hero?

Profile of Judit Polgár

1 → My sporting hero is Judit Polgár. She's 15 and she's from Budapest in Hungary. She's got long brown hair and brown eyes.

2 → Judit's a chess player. She's young, but she's already the number one female chess player of all time and the youngest Grandmaster of all time.

3 → Good chess players have to think quickly and have a fantastic memory. Judit plays really well, and I admire her because she can play against the best players and win.

Anna Simons, March 1992

3 a Read the tips in the HOW TO box.

  b Read the profile of Judit Polgár again. Write the number of the paragraph (1–3) next to the correct information.

    _____ Her skills and why I admire her
    _____ Her sport and her awards
    _____ A description of her

PRACTISE

4 Divide the description into three paragraphs. Write // at the end of each one.

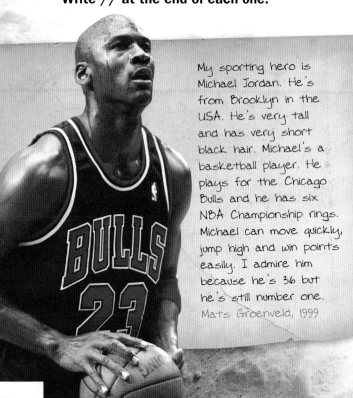

My sporting hero is Michael Jordan. He's from Brooklyn in the USA. He's very tall and has very short black hair. Michael's a basketball player. He plays for the Chicago Bulls and he has six NBA Championship rings. Michael can move quickly, jump high and win points easily. I admire him because he's 36 but he's still number one.

Mats Groenveld, 1999

Get it right

*She's got **a** long hair.* = <u>one</u> long hair
She's got long hair. = <u>all</u> her hair is long

PLAN

5 You're going to write a profile of your sporting hero. Use the *Writing plan* to help you prepare.

WRITING PLAN

1 **Paragraph 1 – Describe your hero.**

  How old is he/she? Where's he/she from? What does he/she look like?

2 **Paragraph 2 – Say why he/she's famous.**

  What sport does he/she play? What are his/her awards?

3 **Paragraph 3 – Say why he/she's your hero.**

  What are his/her skills? Why do you admire him/her?

WRITE AND CHECK

6 Write your profile. Then check it. Tick (✓) the things in the plan.

SHARE

7 Swap your profile with other students. Who's the class's number one sporting hero?

VOCABULARY Sports and games

1 Match the pictures (1–12) to the sports and games in the box.

____ American football	____ badminton
____ bowling	____ cards
____ chess	____ cricket
____ gymnastics	____ ice hockey
____ rugby	____ skateboarding
____ snowboarding	____ video games

GAMES AND
SPORTS
AT THE FIVE STAR CLUB

___ /12

Games verbs

2 Complete the verbs.

IN OUR ★★★★★
VIDEO GAMES ROOM YOU CAN . . .

… (1) cl_____ over walls and
(2) j_____ between buildings in a virtual city.
… (3) l_____ f_____ aliens in space and,
when you find them, (4) sh_____ and
(5) de_____ them.
… (6) m_____ your pieces around a digital
chess board in a game against our computer.
… (7) w_____ or (8) l_____ a game of
tennis against your favourite star.
… (9) th_____ or (10) h_____ the ball in a
game of baseball.

___ /10

GRAMMAR Can/can't for ability; adverbs of manner

3 Write complete sentences and questions with can and an adverb.

READ WHAT OUR MEMBERS SAY!

1 you / think / quick?
If not, join the Five Star Chess Club!

2 We / book / a football pitch / easy.
We just go to the club's website.

3 On weekdays / my son / not get up / early.
But he loves getting up for football training!

4 I / play / tennis / really good.
Thank you Five Star Club!

5 you / run / fast?
If not, join the club!

6 We / not train / hard.
But we train regularly and we're both 70!

___ /12

Have to and don't have to

4 Complete the conversation with have to, don't have to and short answers.

Drew: Hello, and welcome to the Five Star Club.
Misty: I'd like to use the swimming pool.
(1) _____ (you / be) a member?
Drew: No, you (2) _____. But you
(3) _____ (buy) a day ticket.
However, if you're a friend of a member, it's
free and you (4) _____ (pay).
Misty: My friend Helen's a member.
(5) _____ (she / come) with me?
Drew: Yes, she (6) _____. But she
(7) _____ (go) swimming.
She can watch you. Oh, and remember
to bring a swimming cap. All swimmers
(8) _____ (wear) a cap.

___ /16

Your score: ___ /50

SKILLS CHECK

✓✓✓	Yes, I can. No problem!
✓✓	Yes, I can. But I need a bit of help.
✓	Yes, I can. But I need a lot of help.

I can understand new words when I read. ____
I can understand spoken instructions. ____
I can work with others in a team. ____
I can ask for and give or refuse permission. ____
I can use paragraphs. ____

READ

1 **Complete the five conversations. For each question, choose A, B or C.**

Example:

0   *What's your favourite food?*

    A   *Tea with milk.*

    (B)   *Pasta with sauce.*

    C   *Lunch.*

1   *We have to decide as a team.*

    A   *I can't play football.*

    B   *I like sports.*

    C   *Yes, you're right.*

2   *Can I go to Bart's house?*

    A   *Yes, he can.*

    B   *Of course.*

    C   *No, you aren't.*

3   *My dad's got a new job at the hospital.*

    A   *That's fantastic.*

    B   *That's terrible.*

    C   *I'm sorry.*

4   *Are there any cheese sandwiches?*

    A   *Yes, please.*

    B   *Yes, here you are.*

    C   *I don't like chicken.*

5   *Can you play cricket?*

    A   *Yes, I can but I don't really like it.*

    B   *Really?*

    C   *I think plays are boring.*

Reading: _____ /10

EXAM TIPS

 answer multiple-choice questions

- Look at the example. It shows you what to do.
- Read each question and the three answer choices.
- Decide which choices are definitely wrong.
  - Does the meaning of the answer match the question?
  - Does the grammar in the answer match the question? (Look at pronouns, tenses, etc.)
- Read the question again and check your answer.

react to news
See page 61

ask for and give or refuse permission
See page 71

LISTEN

2 ▶**2.40** **Listen to Greg talking about sports and games. Which sports or games do the people in his family do? For questions 1–5, write A–H next to each person.**

Example:

0 sister   *D*

PEOPLE	SPORTS AND GAMES
	A gymnastics
1 brother	**B** video games
2 mum	**C** badminton
3 dad	**D** skateboarding
4 grandma	**E** snowboarding
5 aunt	**F** cards
	G chess
	H football

Listening: _____ /10

WRITE

3 **Complete Galina's profile of her friend. For questions 1–10, write one word for each gap.**

My best friend's name
(0) _____*is*_____ Nika. Nika
(1) _____ in the flat
next door to me. She's
(2) _____ two brothers
and a sister. Nika likes
(3) _____ to music and
(4) _____ TV. She hasn't
got (5) _____ video
games. She (6) _____
like playing video games
(7) _____ she thinks
they're boring.
Nika is good at most sports but
she (8) _____ swim very
well. She has (9) _____
go to swimming lessons every
Saturday (10) _____ her
little brother.

Writing: _____ /10

Progress check score _____ /30

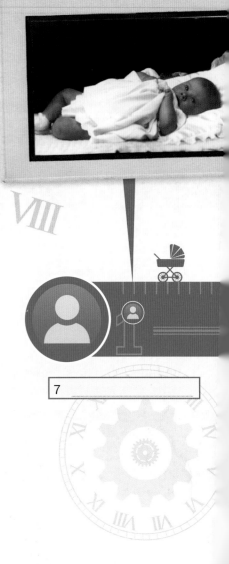

UNIT 7

TIMELINES

IN THE PICTURE A timeline

>>> Talk about people's lives

WORK WITH WORDS Times of life

1 a **RECALL** Work in pairs. Say the dates to your partner. Use the table for help with the year. You have three minutes.

15/06/2002

The fifteenth of June, two thousand and two.

1 21/08/1845
2 15/04/1912
3 31/12/1999
4 01/01/2000
5 12/12/2013

Write	Say
1902	Nineteen oh two
1975	Nineteen seventy-five
2000	Two thousand
2009	Two thousand and nine
2010	Twenty ten

b Check how to say the dates on page 142.

2 a Look at the timeline of Jack's life. Work in pairs. Complete the timeline with the words in the box.

baby   child   middle-aged   pensioner   teenager   young adult

b ▶2.41 Listen and check. Complete the timeline (1–6) with the correct ages.

3 ▶2.41 Listen again. Complete the timeline gaps (7–10) with the verbs in the box.

be born   die   get old   grow up

4 ▶2.42 Listen and repeat the words in exercises 2a and 3.

5 a Write the time of life for the descriptions.

Description	Time of life
1 is in the first 12 years of life	c h i l d
2 is old and doesn't work	
3 was born a few weeks or months ago	
4 is growing up and is nearly an adult	
5 isn't a child or teenager now	
6 isn't old but is getting old	-

b Work in pairs. Say an age. Your partner says the time of life.

6 **THE MOVING PICTURE** ▶ Watch the video. Answer the questions.

1 What's the person's face and hair like at different times of life?
2 How does it change?
3 What clothes is the person wearing at different times?

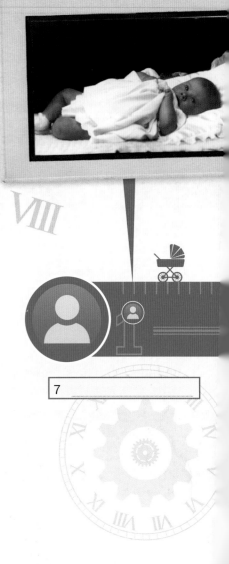

1 ....
Age ▮

7 ....

2 ....
Age ☐

3 ....
Age ☐

4 ....
Age ☐

5 ....
Age ☐

6 ....
Age ☐

8 ....

9 ....

10 ....

WRITE AND SPEAK

7 a Complete the form for a friend or somebody in your family.

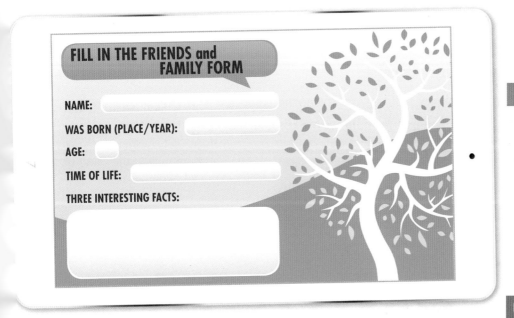

FILL IN THE FRIENDS and
FAMILY FORM

NAME:

WAS BORN (PLACE/YEAR):

AGE:

TIME OF LIFE:

THREE INTERESTING FACTS:

 PHRASE BYTES

I want to tell you about …
He/She was born in …
He's/She's …

 GO BEYOND

Do the Words & Beyond
exercises on page 136.

b 🔊 **Work in pairs. Tell your partner about your person.**

SPEAK AND READ

1 a Work in pairs. Look at the photos. Which things did people have in the year 1000? Tick (✓) them.

1☐ 2☐ 3☐ 4☐ 5☐ 6☐

b 😊 What do you think life was like for people in 1000?

2 ▶2.43 Read the history book information. Check your answers from Exercise 1.

LIFE IN ENGLAND IN THE YEAR 1000

What was life like in England over a thousand years ago? Well, there weren't many people – between two and three million (today there are over 53 million). There weren't many towns and home for 90% of English people was the country. Their houses were **simple** with only one or two rooms. We know that food was healthy because people were quite tall (men were about 172cm) and their teeth were good. There were usually two meals a day – with knives and spoons but no forks. A typical meal was bread with eggs, cheese or fish. There wasn't much meat and there was no sugar, tea, coffee or chocolate.

But life in the 11th **century** wasn't easy. Most people were poor farmers and work in the **fields** was hard. A lot of people were hungry in the summer months before the harvest. When people were ill, there weren't any hospitals or **medicine**. Adults were usually dead before they were 40 and babies were often dead before their first birthday.

As their lives were short, people were married when they were teenagers – girls from when they were 12 and boys from 14. In poor families children were field workers like the adults. **Education** was only for the rich.

3 a Read the tips in the HOW TO box.

b Read again. Choose the best match for the words in bold.

1	simple	**A** very big	**B** with not many parts	**C** with new furniture
2	century	**A** 10 years	**B** 100 years	**C** 1,000 years
3	field	**A** house	**B** town	**C** piece of land
4	medicine	**A** it makes you better	**B** it makes you tired	**C** it makes you happy
5	education	**A** eating	**B** working	**C** learning

4 Which tips in the HOW TO box did you use for help with Exercise 3b? Tick (✓) them.

5 Find these numbers in the text. Write what they mean.

1 between 2 and 3 million   *people in England in the year 1000*
2 53 million   _____
3 90%   _____
4 172cm   _____
5 40   _____
6 12   _____

REACT

6 Work in pairs. Make two lists: what was good and bad in the year 1000? What's good and bad today?

>>> **Talk about situations in the past**

READ AND LISTEN >>> Grammar in context

1 ▶2.44 **Read and listen to the conversation. Who was born in the year 2000?**

Jamal:	Where were you born? Were you born here in Liverpool?
Dakota:	No, I wasn't. I was born in London – 13 years ago.
Jamal:	Was your sister born in London too?
Dakota:	Yes, she was. She was born in 2000 – on January 1st at 1am!
Jamal:	Wow! That was a great time to be born! There were big parties everywhere.
Dakota:	Yes. But my mum and dad weren't at a party – they were at the hospital!

STUDY

2 **Complete the explanations with the correct words. Use Exercise 1 to help you.**

Was/were; ago

Use: To talk about situations in the past.

Form:

Positive and negative
I/he/she/it + _____ /wasn't
we/you/they + were/ _____

Questions and short answers
_____ he/she/it ... ?
Yes, she was. / No, I _____ .
Were we/you/they ... ?
Yes, they were. / No, they weren't.

Time expressions:
time period + *ago*
I was born thirteen years ago.
See GRAMMAR DATABASE, page 126.

✅ **Get it right**

Use *at* with places: *at school/home/work, at (Amira)'s house, at the baker's/doctor's, at the cinema/shopping centre, at a party/concert/hotel.*

Use *in* with cities/towns and countries and rooms (*in my bedroom*).

PRACTISE

3 **Choose the correct word.**

For the new millennium there (1) *was* / were celebrations around the world. But they (2) *wasn't* / *weren't* just parties. Opening new buildings (3) *was* / *wasn't* a part of these celebrations too. There (4) *was* / *were* new millennium towers in Vienna and Abu Dhabi, and the London Eye big wheel in London. People (5) *wasn't* / *weren't* sure about the London Eye at first but it (6) *was* / *wasn't* soon very popular.

4 a **Write the questions.**

1 Where / you / on December 31st three years ago?
Where were you on December 31st three years ago?   d
2 Which school / you at two years ago?
3 Where / you on holiday a year ago?
4 Who / you with four hours ago?
5 Where / you an hour ago?

b **Complete Jamal's answers with *at* or *in*. Then match them to the questions in Exercise 4a.**

a I was with my friends _____ the cinema.
b I was _____ my bedroom _____ home.
c I was _____ this school.
d I was _____ a party _____ my cousin's house.
e We were _____ a hotel _____ Turkey.

WRITE AND SPEAK

5 a **Write the answers to the questions in Exercise 4a for you.**

b **Work in pairs. Ask and answer the questions with your partner. Think of two more questions.**

Where were you on December 31st three years ago?

I was at home with my family.

I can't remember!

SPEAK AND LISTEN

1 a **Look at the pictures from two books for teenagers. Then read the tips in the HOW TO box.**

b ⊙ **Work in pairs. Student A: Look at picture 1. Student B: Look at picture 2. Tell your partner what you can see. What are the books about?**

2 ▶2.45 **Listen to parts of the books. Check your answers from Exercise 1b.**

3 **Which tips in the HOW TO box did you use for help with Exercise 2? Tick (✓) them.**

4 ▶2.45 **Listen again. Put the events in the correct order (1–5).**

> **Amelia's story**
> _____ Emma's baby was born.
> _____ Amelia's family talked about their new life.
> _____ The family's cow died.
> _1_ Amelia's family started to walk to Oregon from Missouri.
> _____ They **bought** some clothes from the Indians.

> **William's story**
> _____ Josephine and William **went** for a walk and **had** a wonderful day.
> _____ William **met** Josephine.
> _____ The ship stopped in Ireland.
> _1_ The ship **left** England.
> _____ Josephine **told** William about New York.

5 **Match the verbs below to the correct past simple forms in bold in Exercise 4.**

1 tell _____   3 go _____   5 buy _____
2 leave _____   4 meet _____   6 have _____

REACT

6 **Work in pairs. Did you enjoy listening to the books? How do you feel now?**

I really enjoyed …

WORK WITH WORDS **Personality adjectives**

7 **Match the adjectives (1–5) to the people in the listening.**

1 **nice** (easy to like)
2 **cheerful** (happy)
3 **serious** (doesn't usually laugh much)
4 **friendly** (wanted to help)
5 **shy** (doesn't like talking to new people)

8 **Read these sentences. Which two words in bold are opposites?**

1 I like Amelia and William. I think they're **cool**.
2 Amelia doesn't get angry, she's very **calm**.
3 She's very **polite** and always says 'thank you'.
4 William is very **funny**; he makes Josephine laugh.
5 William isn't **rude**; he always opens doors for people.

9 ▶2.46 **Listen and repeat the words in bold in exercises 7 and 8.**

10 **Work in pairs. Describe famous people with words from exercises 7 and 8. Does your partner agree?**

I think … is very shy.   *Yes, you're right.*

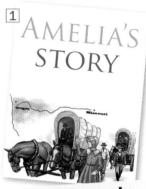

William's story

I feel sad because …

_____ Amelia's family
_____ the Indians
_____ the Bloomberg Family
_____ Josephine
_____ Josephine

> **HOW TO** ❓
> use pictures to help you listen
>
> ☐ Look at the style. Is it old or modern?
>
> ☐ Look at the people. How old are they? Are they family or friends? What are they doing? How do they feel?
>
> ☐ Look at the place. Where is it? (Inside or outside? In a town or in the country?, etc)

> **GO BEYOND**
>
> Do the Words & Beyond exercise on page 136.

>>> **Talk about completed events in the past**

READ >>> Grammar in context

1 Read Jada's diary. Was this day a special day?

13 ———— DECEMBER 2012

Dear Diary,

Yesterday was the 12th of December 2012 (12.12.12) and the Mayan Calendar finished. Years ago, some people said this day was the end of the world. But nothing happened! Nothing changed. At school I saw my friends, did lessons and ate lunch. Then I played basketball. After dinner I watched TV, got some messages and wrote to my friends. Another normal day!

STUDY

2 a **Complete the explanation. Use Exercise 1 to help you.**

Past simple positive

Use: For completed actions in the past.

Form:

Regular verbs
verb + _____
I/he/she/it/we/you/they finish**ed**

Irregular verbs
Learn the past simple forms (*was – were, say – said*) on page 126.

Time expressions:
yesterday, last week/month/year, a week/years ago
See GRAMMAR DATABASE, page 126.

b **In Exercise 1, <u>underline</u> four more regular verbs and circle five more irregular verbs.**

PRACTISE

3 **Complete the sentences from Jada's diary. Use the correct past simple form of the regular verbs.**

1 I _____ (walk) home with Ivan after school.

2 My mum _____ (cook) my favourite meal.

3 I _____ (love) my English class today.

4 My little brother _____ (cry) all evening.

5 Lucy and I _____ (chat) online.

6 My friends _____ (want) to go shopping.

>>> Workbook, page 86

4 a ▶2.47 **PRONOUNCE** **Listen to the -ed ending in these verbs. Listen and repeat.**

changed /d/   finished /t/   chatted /ɪd/

b ▶2.48 **Listen to these past simple forms. Circle the correct sound: /d/, /t/ or /ɪd/.**

		/d/	/t/	/ɪd/
1	wanted	/d/	/t/	/ɪd/
2	happened	/d/	/t/	/ɪd/
3	watched	/d/	/t/	/ɪd/
4	walked	/d/	/t/	/ɪd/
5	played	/d/	/t/	/ɪd/
6	needed	/d/	/t/	/ɪd/

5 a **Match the two parts of Jada's sentences.**

IMPORTANT EVENTS IN MY LIFE

1 Five years ago we **got**
2 In 2013 I **met**
3 Two years ago my parents **bought** me
4 On holiday in Norway last year we **saw**
5 Last week I **had**
6 Yesterday my big sister **left**

a my favourite singer.
b my 13th birthday.
c home.
d my first phone.
e our cat.
f the Northern Lights.

b **Write the verbs for the past simple forms in Exercise 5a. Check your answers on page 140.**

6 **Complete the conversation with the correct past simple form of the verbs.**

Marco: Yesterday I (1) _____ (have) a great day. We (2) _____ (do) a test and my answers (3) _____ (be) all right. We (4) _____ (go) to a café for dinner. And I (5) _____ (talk) to Beth on the phone. What about you?

Jada: Another normal day. I (6) _____ (write) the wrong answers in my homework. We (7) _____ (eat) toast for dinner. And my phone (8) _____ (die).

SPEAK

7 **Work in pairs. Tell your partner about your day yesterday.**

Yesterday I met some friends.

I started my history project.

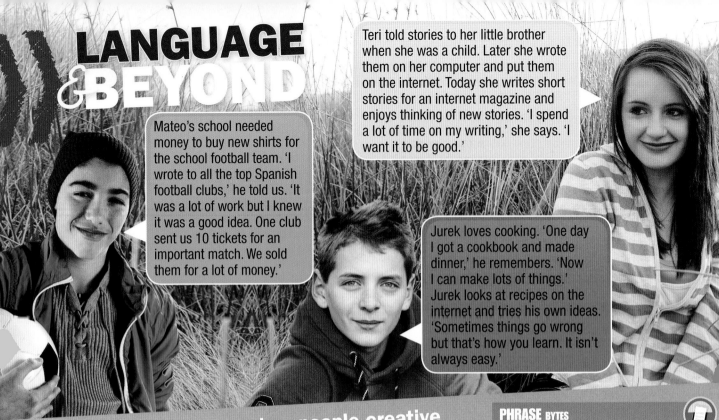

LANGUAGE & BEYOND

Mateo's school needed money to buy new shirts for the school football team. 'I wrote to all the top Spanish football clubs,' he told us. 'It was a lot of work but I knew it was a good idea. One club sent us 10 tickets for an important match. We sold them for a lot of money.'

Teri told stories to her little brother when she was a child. Later she wrote them on her computer and put them on the internet. Today she writes short stories for an internet magazine and enjoys thinking of new stories. 'I spend a lot of time on my writing,' she says. 'I want it to be good.'

Jurek loves cooking. 'One day I got a cookbook and made dinner,' he remembers. 'Now I can make lots of things.' Jurek looks at recipes on the internet and tries his own ideas. 'Sometimes things go wrong but that's how you learn. It isn't always easy.'

>>> Understand what makes people creative

GET THINKING

SPEAK AND READ

1 ◉ **Make a class list of famous creative people. In what way are they creative?**

2 ◉ **Read the descriptions above of three creative teenagers. In what way are they creative?**

DO

3 **Creative people all share the things below. Underline examples in the descriptions of Mateo, Teri and Jurek.**
   - They have new ideas, try new things or do things in new ways.
   - They really love their hobby or believe in their idea.
   - They work hard.

4 a **Work in small groups. Choose ONE task from the box.**

   b **Share your ideas with another group.**

REFLECT

5 **Talk about the questions. Then read the (REFLECTION POINT).**
   1 Was your task in Exercise 4a easy or difficult? In what ways were you creative?
   2 Do you think you're creative? Why?/Why not? Is your opinion different after Exercise 4a?
   3 What stops people being creative?

EXTEND

6 **Tell a partner three ways you're creative.**

   I thought of a new way to learn English vocabulary.
   I have a blog with photos of clothes.
   I made a poster for a school party.

PHRASE BYTES

He/She was a painter / guitar player / computer designer …

He/She wrote / made / designed / had the idea for …

He's/She's a writer / website designer …

He/She makes films / writes songs …

SHOW HOW CREATIVE YOU ARE!

- Make a story with these words:
  said   ship   cards   cinema
  met   cried   calm

- Write a new menu for school lunch or a meal for a special day.

- Think of ideas to get money for new books for your school.

REFLECTION POINT

Everyone can be creative in big or small ways. You can make something, do something in a different way or have a new idea. Work hard to make your ideas real.

SPEAKING Guess what?

SPEAK

1  **Work in pairs. Look at the photos. What kind of story are Joe and Rose telling?**

Joe/Rose is telling a sad/funny/strange/boring/interesting … story.

Joe and Amy are …

Rose/Luca looks …

WATCH OR LISTEN

2 a ▶︎▶︎**2.49** **Watch or listen to the scenes. Check your answers to Exercise 1.**

1

Joe:	Guess (1) _____ ?
Amy:	What?
Joe:	I went shopping with Mum yesterday. When we were in the supermarket, we were behind that new teacher – you (2) _____ , she's got long, dark hair. She does the healthy eating lessons.
Amy:	Oh, yes.
Joe:	(3) _____ , I looked in her shopping basket. There were no vegetables or fruit. She bought two pizzas, a big cake and lots of chocolate!

2

Rose:	Know (4) _____ ?
Luca:	What?
Rose:	Yesterday I was at home in my room. My parents were in the garden. (5) _____ , I was on my computer and my phone rang. I answered it and somebody said 'I love you'.
Luca:	And then?
Rose:	That was it. I don't know who it was. It was really (6) _____ .

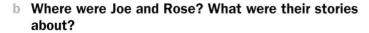

b **Where were Joe and Rose? What were their stories about?**

3 ▶︎▶︎**2.49** **Watch or listen again. Complete Joe and Rose's stories with the words in the box. Then listen to the phrases again and check.**

anyway	know	strange	well	what (x2)

4 ▶︎**2.50** **Listen and repeat the phrases in Exercise 3.**

5 **We use *Guess what?* or *(Do you) know what?* to start an interesting or funny story. Which word or phrase is the answer to both questions? Find it in the conversations.**

ACT

6 a  **Work in pairs. Look at the picture story on page 141 or think of your own story. Practise telling the story.**

b **Present your story to another pair.**

PHRASEBOOK ▶︎**2.51**

TELLING A STORY
Create interest
Guess what?
(Do you) know what?

Explain what happened
Yesterday I went shopping / to the cinema …
I was in the supermarket / my room …
My teacher / Somebody / My friend bought/said …
… , you know, …

Continue with the story
Well, … / Anyway, …

Make a comment
It was really strange/funny …

WRITING My diary

SPEAK AND READ

1 🔊 **Work in pairs. Do you write in a diary or a blog? What do you write about? Tell the class.**

2 **Read Paco's blog. What was good about his week? What was bad?**

PACO'S BLOG

Home   About   Contact   Search

24th November

How was your week?

This was a good and bad week for me. Guess what? Yesterday I had my 13th birthday. We went to my favourite ice-cream place after school and we had a special dinner later. I can't wait for my party on Saturday!

On Monday evening our school basketball team lost 15–12. (We lost 18–3 last Monday!) But I got 20 out of 20 in my vocabulary test this morning.

3 a **Read the tips in the HOW TO box.**

HOW TO

use time expressions

- Use expressions like *yesterday, after school, on Monday, last Monday* and *this morning* to say when something happened.

- Use *later* to write about a time after another time.

- Put the time expression at the end of the sentence (normal word order).

- Put the time expression at the start of the sentence to emphasise the time.

b **Underline a different example for each tip in Paco's blog.**

✅ **Get it right**

We can use some time expressions like *after school, on Monday* and *this morning* for both past and future times.

PRACTISE

4 **Read Paco's next blog entry a week later. Rewrite it with these time expressions.**

- after dinner ▪ last week ▪ later
- on Saturday evening

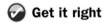

Sorry – I was very busy! We had my birthday party. My parents watched TV upstairs and my friends and I listened to music and danced. We watched a film.

PLAN

5 **You're going to write your diary or blog for last week. Use the *Writing plan* to help you prepare.**

WRITING PLAN

1 **Say if it was a good or bad week.**
   What was the most important thing? When did it happen?

2 **Say what else happened.**
   When? Why was it good or bad?

3 **Say what you can't wait to do soon.**
   What are your plans for later this week?

4 **Remember to use time expressions.**
   Look at the tips in the HOW TO box.

WRITE AND CHECK

6 **Write your diary or blog. Then check it. Tick (✓) the things in the plan.**

SHARE

7 **Swap your diary or blog entry with other students. Who had a really good or really bad week?**

VOCABULARY Times of life

1 Complete the sentences with the words in the box.

> adult   baby   born   child   die   get
> grow up   middle-aged   pensioner   teenager

Home | Creative cards | Gifts | Contact us ✉

Do you need **a card** for a **special day**?
We've got cards for **everything** and **everybody**!

When a little (1) _____ is
(2) _____ .
When a (3) _____ is five or six.
Cards with '13' for (4) _____ s.
When you (5) _____ : Lots of cards for
(6) _____ s in their 20s and 30s.
Cards with '40' and '50' for (7) _____
friends.
Nobody likes to (8) _____ old. We have
nice cards for (9) _____ s.
And for when old people (10) _____
and you feel sad.

___ /10

Personality adjectives

2 Complete the personality words.

Choose the **right card** for the **right person**

(1) c_____ l kids 😎
(2) sh_____ boys 😊
(3) ni_____ girls 😊
(4) fu_____ y friends 😄
(5) c_____ m parents 😊
(6) fr_____ dly grandparents 😀
(7) ser_____ s uncles 😐
(8) ch_____ ful teachers 😄
All our cards have nice, (9) po_____
messages
We don't have (10) r_____ e cards

GOOD
LUCK

HAVE A
NICE
DAY

Thank
You

___ /10

GRAMMAR Was/were

3 Choose the correct word for the card messages.

Thank you. You (1) was / were a great teacher.

Wow! That (2) was / wasn't a fantastic idea!

I (3) was / were horrible to you. But you (4) wasn't / weren't angry. Thanks.

Thank You

It (5) was / were a cool party.
I (6) wasn't / weren't bored for one minute!

___ /14

You (7) was / were my first love. ♡

Past simple positive

4 Complete the conversation with the correct past simple form of the verbs.

Blake: I (1) _____ (get) a birthday card from
my uncle today. He (2) _____ (design)
it himself and he (3) _____ (write) a
really nice message. It (4) _____ (say)
'I (5) _____ (forget) your birthday last
year. But I (6) _____ (look) in my diary
this year and I (7) _____ (remember).'

Yakira: That's nice. But it (8) _____ (be) your
birthday last week.

___ /16

Your score: ___ /50

SKILLS CHECK

✓✓✓	Yes, I can. No problem!
✓✓	Yes, I can. But I need a bit of help.
✓	Yes, I can. But I need a lot of help.

I can understand new words in a text. _____
I can use pictures to help me listen. _____
I can understand what makes people creative. _____
I can tell an interesting or funny story. _____
I can use time expressions when I write. _____

ON THE MOVE

IN THE PICTURE My travel blog

>>> **Talk about places and the weather**

WORK WITH WORDS Weather and prepositions of movement

1 a (RECALL) **Work in pairs. Write adjectives for the nouns. You have one minute.**

1 cloud *cloudy*
2 fog _____
3 rain _____
4 snow _____
5 sun _____
6 wind _____

b Complete the adjectives.

1 c_____
2 w_____
3 h_____

2 Work in pairs. Describe the weather in the photos. Use the words in Exercise 1.

3 ▶3.01 **Listen to the audio blogs (1–5) and match them to the photos (b–f).**

4 a Label the icons (a–j) with the prepositions of movement in the box.

around   down   into   out of   up

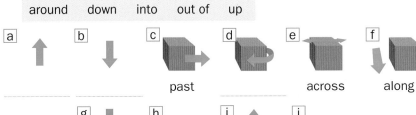

a   b   c _____ past   d _____   e across   f along

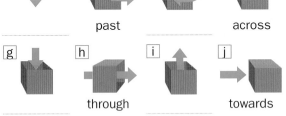

g _____ through   h   i   j towards

b ▶3.02 **Listen and check. Then listen and repeat.**

5 ▶3.01 **Complete the blog entries with the correct prepositions from Exercise 4. Then listen and check.**

6 Look at the photo of the signpost. What's unusual about it? Where do you think it is?

Signposts usually show …

This one shows …

📎 **MY TRAVEL BLOG**　　　Home　**Blog**　About　Subscribe

Posted Wednesday 21st

1 On the second day we took a lift and went _____ to the top of the Empire State Building. The weather was really bad. We couldn't see anything through the fog. So we came _____ after about two minutes!

2 Today we walked _____ the Monteverde Cloud Forest. It was amazing. In this photo we're looking at some birds in the trees.

3 This is my grandma and my brother. They're walking _____ a street in the Marais district of Paris, _____ some shops.

4 In this photo I'm looking _____ the tent. It's sunny but some clouds are moving _____ the sky. They're coming _____ me!

5 It rained all day, but we had a good time and the music was great. We walked _____ the festival area and then went _____ the tents to get out of the rain.

Like　Comments

HOME   CHAT

Pole 3 hrs. 15 min.

penhagen 4 hrs. 15 min.

Los Angeles 6 hrs. 45min.

New York 4 hrs.

5 hrs. 20 min.

7 **THE MOVING PICTURE** ▶ **Watch the video and describe what you see. What's the weather like? What are the people doing? Use the prepositions from Exercise 4.**

SPEAK

8 Work in pairs. Complete the tasks.

1 Draw a signpost like the one in the photo. Use the names of places in or near your school.
2 Take it in turns to ask for directions to one of the places.
3 Give directions using the prepositions in Exercise 4. How many prepositions can you use?

> *How do I get to … ?*

> *Go through the door, walk along …*

> *Go out of the school …*

GO BEYOND »

Do the Words & Beyond exercise on page 137.

»» Workbook, page 92

READING A cool place to visit

SPEAK AND READ

1 Work in pairs. Answer the questions.

1 What can you see in the photos of Istanbul?
2 What do you know about Istanbul? Write three facts.

2 a Read the tips in the HOW TO box.

b ▶3.03 Read Sara's travel blog. Did she have a good time, an OK time or a bad time?

HOW TO

identify the writer's opinion

☐ Look for words meaning *good* or *bad*: *great, terrible* … .

☐ Look for *be* and *like*: *It was/ wasn't* … , *I liked / didn't like* … .

☐ Look for these phrases: *I think / don't think* … .

🎒 MY TRAVEL BLOG

Home **Blog** About Subscribe

Posted Monday 21st

Istanbul

Last month I went with my family to Turkey. We flew by plane from Toronto to Istanbul. The flight took 11 hours! It was very boring and I couldn't sleep. At the airport we got into a taxi and drove (very fast) to the hotel. The hotel was OK but it wasn't fantastic.
The next day I woke up very early and we had breakfast. There were eggs, some bread, yoghurt, tomatoes and cheese. It was different but I liked it.
After breakfast we walked into the centre and looked around the city. The weather was terrible. It was cold and windy. We did some sightseeing and I had a great time. We visited the Sultan Ahmed Mosque (the Blue Mosque), which was BIG!!! I took millions of photos outside.
In the afternoon we walked through the Grand Bazaar (it's got 3,000 shops!). It was an amazing place but I didn't buy anything. I don't speak Turkish but a lot of people could understand English. I think Turkey is a very cool place to visit. I had a great time and I'd like to go back one day.

3 What was Sara's opinion of these things? Tick (✓) the correct box in the table on the right.

4 Which tips in the HOW TO box did you use for help with exercises 2b and 3? Tick (✓) them.

5 Order the activities in Sara's blog.

..... We walked through the bazaar.
..... I took millions of photos.
..... We flew to Istanbul.
..... I had breakfast.

..... We visited the mosque.
..... We got a taxi to the hotel.
..... We walked into the centre.

	good	OK	bad
flight			
hotel			
breakfast			
weather			
sightseeing			
Grand Bazaar			

REACT

6 Work in pairs. What do you think? Tell your partner.

1 Which three cities would you like to visit in the world? Why would you like to visit them?
2 Choose one city and tell the class about it.

We'd like to go to …
  because …   *We think … is a(n) … place.*

GO BEYOND

Make a list of the things to see and do in one of the other cities you chose in Exercise 6.

READ >>> Grammar in context

**1 Read the email message.
Why is Ravi happy to be home?**

New mail ← Reply → Forward	✕

Hi! I'm sorry I didn't call you last week. I was on holiday with my family. I didn't have a great time. As you can see in the photo, the weather wasn't good so we didn't do much. I didn't like the hotel but there was a games room, so we could play table tennis. On the third day I didn't feel well, so I didn't get out of bed all day. And I couldn't eat any food. It's nice to be home!

Ravi

STUDY

2 a Complete the explanations with examples in Exercise 1.

Past simple negative

Use: For describing things that didn't happen in the past.

Form:

Negative

I/you, etc + *didn't* + verb:
We _____ .

I/you, etc + *wasn't/weren't*:
The weather _____ .

I/you, etc + *couldn't* + verb:
I _____ .

See GRAMMAR DATABASE, page 127.

b Underline more examples of the negative past simple in Exercise 1.

PRACTISE

3 a What did Ravi's family do when he was ill in bed? Write sentences in the past simple.

1 Ravi's brother / go / to the shops.
   Ravi's brother went to the shops.
2 His mum and dad / walk / around the town.
3 Ravi's sister / dance / at the disco.
4 Mum / take / lots of photos.
5 They all / eat / pizzas for lunch.
6 'We / have / an amazing time.'

b Write the sentences in Exercise 3a about Ravi in the past simple negative.

Ravi was in bed so …
1 he didn't go to the shops.

4 Choose the correct words in Ravi's story.

On the last day of the holiday I felt OK so I (1) *could / couldn't* get out of bed. It (2) *wasn't / was* very late so I couldn't have breakfast. Dad was really nice. He (3) *drove / didn't drive* us around the island. When we came back it was late so the shops (4) *were / weren't* closed. But I (5) *couldn't / could* eat pizza again so it (6) *was / wasn't* all bad!

5 ▶3.04 Look at the advert and complete the conversation. Then listen and check.

COME TO OUR HOTEL!

- It has a swimming pool.
- The beaches are beautiful.
- The weather is always sunny.
- You can visit the theme park.
- We have tour guides to help you.

IT'S CHEAP!

Sonia: Hi Ravi. How was the holiday?
Ravi: It was terrible. All the information in the advert was wrong.
The hotel (1) *didn't have a swimming pool* .
The beaches (2) _____ .
The weather (3) _____ .
We (4) _____ .
The tour guides (5) _____ .
And the holiday (6) _____ !

SPEAK

6 Work in pairs. Talk to your partner about your last holiday. Find three things that you both did.

I stayed at a hotel.

I didn't stay at a hotel. I took some photos.

Me too! / I didn't take any photos. I …

>>> **Take notes**

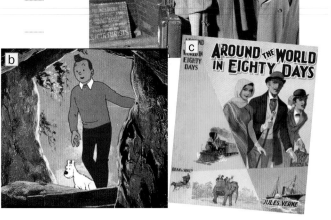

SPEAK AND LISTEN

1 **Work in pairs. Match the sentences (1–3) to the pictures (a–c).**

1 Phileas Fogg is a character in a novel by Jules Verne.
2 Palle Huld was a Danish schoolboy. He became famous in 1928, aged 15 years old.
3 Tintin and his dog, Snowy, are characters in a series of comic books by Hergé.

2 a **Read the tips in the HOW TO box.**

b **▶3.05 Listen to the radio programme about Palle Huld and take notes. What's the connection between Palle Huld, Jules Verne and Tintin?**

3 **▶3.05 Listen again and complete your notes. Then work in pairs. How many facts do you have about Palle Huld?**

4 **Which tips in the HOW TO box did you use for help with exercises 2b and 3? Tick (✓) them.**

5 **▶3.06 PRONOUNCE We stress the important words in a sentence. Listen and repeat these sentences. Stress the underlined words.**

1 He <u>had</u> to <u>complete</u> the <u>trip</u> in <u>46</u> <u>days</u>.
2 He <u>became</u> an <u>actor</u> and <u>died</u> in <u>2010</u>.

REACT

6 **Work in pairs. Would you like to travel around the world like Palle Huld? Why?/Why not?**

HOW TO ❓

take notes

☐ Listen for the important information – *Who? What? When? Where?*

☐ Write important words or numbers.

☐ Don't write complete sentences.

WORK WITH WORDS Forms of transport

7 a **Match the pictures (a–j) to the words in the box.**

boat	coach
helicopter	lorry
motorbike	plane
ship	train tram
underground	

b **▶3.07 Listen and check. Then listen and repeat.**

8 **Write the forms of transport in Exercise 7a in the correct group.**

Land	Air	Sea
		boat

✅ **Get it right**

You travel **by** boat, plane, car …
You travel **on** foot.

9 **Work in pairs. Answer the questions.**

1 Which forms of transport do you think Palle used on his trip?
2 Which forms of transport do you usually use? When?
3 Which other forms of transport from the list did you use last year?

GO BEYOND 》

Do the Words & Beyond exercise on page 137.

>>> **Ask and answer questions about the past**

READ AND LISTEN >>> Grammar in context

1 ▶3.08 **Read and listen to the quiz show about the book *Around the World in 80 Days*. How many questions does Laura answer correctly?**

Quizmaster:	You need four correct answers to win a trip around the world! Are you ready?
Laura:	Yes, I am.
Quizmaster:	Question 1: Where did Phileas Fogg start his journey?
Laura:	He started in London.
Quizmaster:	Correct. Did he travel by plane?
Laura:	No, he didn't. He travelled by boat, ship, train and … on an elephant!
Quizmaster:	Correct. Which form of transport did Fogg use first?
Laura:	He travelled by train first.
Quizmaster:	Correct. Who was Fix?
Laura:	He was a detective.
Quizmaster:	Correct! That's four correct answers. Well done, Laura. You win a trip around the world!

STUDY

2 Complete the explanations. Use Exercise 1 to help you.

Past simple questions and short answers

Use: For completed actions in the past.

Form:
Most verbs
did + I/she, etc + verb:
_____ *he travel by plane?*
Yes, he did. / No, he _____ .

be
was/were + I/you, etc:
Who _____ *Fix? Was he a detective?*
Yes, he was. / No, he wasn't.

could
could + I/you, etc + verb:
Could Laura answer all the questions?
Yes, she could. / No, she couldn't.

See GRAMMAR DATABASE, page 127.

PRACTISE

3 Laura is going on her world trip. Complete the questions with the correct form of the words and write the short answers.

1 *Did Laura say* (Laura / say) goodbye to her friends? ✓ *Yes, she did.*
2 _____ (they / give) her a present? ✗ _____
3 _____ (they / be) sad? ✓ _____
4 _____ (she / remember) her passport? ✓ _____
5 _____ (she / can / take) her cat with her? ✗ _____
6 _____ (her dad / take) her to the station? ✗ _____

4 ▶3.09 **Complete the conversation after Laura came home with the correct form of the words. Then listen and check.**

Harry: Hi Laura. (1) _____ (you / have) a good trip?
Laura: Yes, (2) _____ , thanks.
Harry: Where (3) _____ (you / go)?
Laura: I went to lots of different countries. What (4) _____ (you / do) while I was away?
Harry: I stayed at home and studied.
Laura: (5) _____ (you / be) very bored?
Harry: No, (6) _____ . I like studying.

5 a Work in pairs. Student A: Write the questions and answers on page 141. Student B: Write the questions and answers on page 142.

b ▪ **Ask your questions.**
▪ **Answer your partner's questions with the correct answer.**

6 Write four past simple questions about famous people, characters or events.

Did Jules Verne write Robinson Crusoe?
Which sport did Björn Borg play?

SPEAK

7 Work in pairs. Ask and answer the questions you wrote in Exercise 6. How many questions can your partner answer correctly?

Did Jules Verne … ?

No, he didn't. Daniel Defoe wrote it.

Which sport … ?

I don't know. / I think it was tennis.

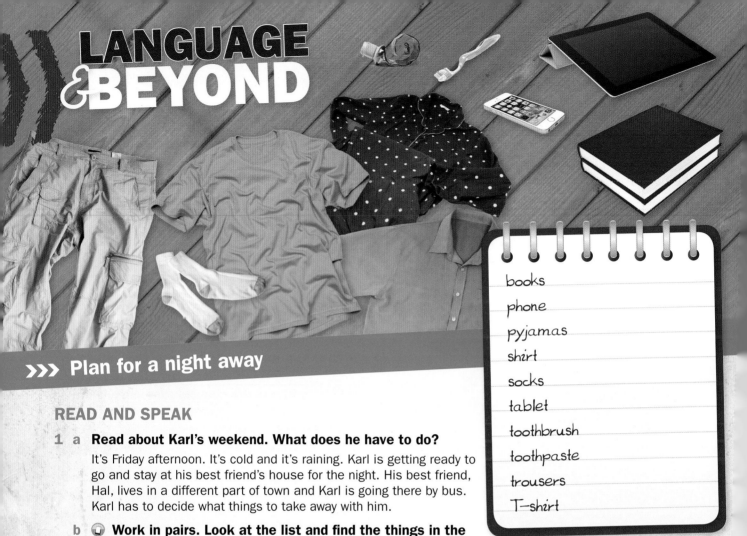

LANGUAGE &BEYOND

books
phone
pyjamas
shirt
socks
tablet
toothbrush
toothpaste
trousers
T-shirt

>>> Plan for a night away

READ AND SPEAK

1 a Read about Karl's weekend. What does he have to do?

It's Friday afternoon. It's cold and it's raining. Karl is getting ready to go and stay at his best friend's house for the night. His best friend, Hal, lives in a different part of town and Karl is going there by bus. Karl has to decide what things to take away with him.

b Work in pairs. Look at the list and find the things in the picture. <u>Underline</u> any new words.

DO

2 Work in groups. What things in Exercise 1b does Karl need?

✓ = important   ? = not very important   ✗ = he doesn't need this

3 Work in pairs. Tick (✓) the important things to think about when you go away.

How long? *one night, two nights, …*
Where? *in a house, a hotel, a tent, …*
Which transport? *by bus, by train, …*
What plans? *go swimming, go to the cinema, …*
What weather? *sunny, rainy, …*

4 Work in pairs. Look at Karl's list again. What other things do you think he needs to take? Add them to the list.

REFLECT

5 Talk about the questions. Then read the REFLECTION POINT.

1 How often do you spend a night away from home?
2 Why is it a good idea to make a list of things to take?
3 What do you need to think about when you make your list?

EXTEND

6 In groups, think of a place to go for a weekend school trip. Make notes about the things to think about in Exercise 3. Then prepare a list of things to take.

> We can go to … and
> stay in/at …

> We can play …

PHRASE BYTES

This is … / These are …
I think this is called …
Where's / Where are … ?

PHRASE BYTES

This is/isn't important because …
He needs / doesn't need to take …
His friend probably has …

REFLECTION POINT

When you spend a night away, remember all the different things you need to think about. Make a list to help you remember.

GET ORGANISED

SPEAKING Check in and out of a hotel

>>> Ask for repetition

LISTEN

1 ▶3.10 **Work in pairs. Listen to Liz on the phone and complete the reservation information.**

NEW RESERVATION ▶

BEYOND HOTEL

Name: _____
Arrival date: _____
Nº nights: _____
Nº rooms & type

SINGLE ☐ TWIN ☐ DOUBLE ☐

WATCH OR LISTEN

2 ▶3.11 **Watch or listen to the scenes. Did Liz, Skye and Alex enjoy their stay at the hotel?**

Alex:	We'd like to check in.
Liz:	We have a reservation.
Receptionist:	One moment, please. What's the name?
Liz:	The reservation's in the name of Finnie.
Receptionist:	One single and one twin room for three nights.
Liz:	That's right.
Receptionist:	Could … sign …
Liz:	I'm sorry?
Receptionist:	I said – (1) _____ ?
Receptionist:	Your rooms are on the third floor.
Skye:	Where are the lifts?
Receptionist:	Go …
Skye:	I'm sorry. Can you repeat that, please?
Receptionist:	Yes. Go (2) _____ the doors, (3) _____ the hall, (4) _____ the breakfast room and they're on the right.
Alex:	Good morning. We'd like to check out, please.
Receptionist:	One moment, please. I … enjoyed …
Alex:	Sorry. What did you say?
Receptionist:	I said – I (5) _____ .
Alex:	Yes, we did, thank you.

3 ▶3.11 **Watch or listen again and write the missing words and phrases.**

4 a **Read the tips in the HOW TO box.**

b **Complete the tasks.**
   1 Find three examples of saying 'sorry' in the conversation.
   2 Find another phrase asking for repetition.

5 a **Complete the PHRASEBOOK with the headings in the box.**

   Ask for repetition   Check in   Check out

b ▶3.12 **Listen and check your answers. Then listen again and repeat.**

ACT

6 **In groups of three or four, do the tasks.**
   1 Choose a location and name for a hotel.
   2 Choose one student to be the hotel receptionist. The others are tourists.
   3 Prepare two short scenes:
      – checking in
      – checking out

HOW TO ❓

ask for repetition

If you don't understand what someone says:

■ be polite. Say: *(I'm) sorry.*

■ ask for repetition: *I'm sorry? Can you repeat that, please?*

PHRASEBOOK ▶3.13

1 _____
I'd/We'd like to check in.
I/We have a reservation.
The reservation's in the name of …
Where are the lifts?

2 _____
We'd like to check out, please.

3 _____
I'm sorry?
Can you repeat that, please?
Sorry. What did you say?

>>> Workbook, page 99

WRITING A message from Mexico

SPEAK AND READ

1 Work in pairs. Answer the questions.

1 Do you have an email address? If so, what do you use email for? If not, why don't you use email?
2 When you write an email, what information do you write at the top?

2 Read the email from Alex and choose the best subject.

A Goodbye Mexico City!
B My first day in Mexico City
C The weather in Mexico City

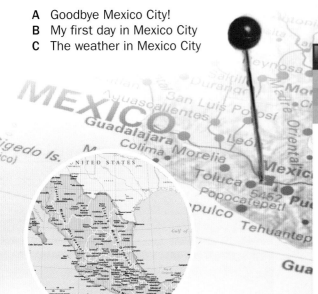

> **HOW TO** ❓
> use descriptive language
> - Use adjectives (*big, amazing* …).
> - Use adverbs (*late, perfectly* …).
> - Add details (*how, when, where, why, who*) and opinions (*I think* …).

✉ New mail ← Reply → Forward ✕

From: Alex Prentice
To: Jamie_Watson@beyondmall.net
Subject:

Hello from Mexico City! We arrived late last night after a long flight. This city is very BIG and LOUD! This morning we went from the hotel to the Zócalo, the main square, by taxi. There's a really big Mexican flag there and an amazing cathedral. The people here are very friendly and I think the food is great (but very hot!). We had lunch in a market. I spoke some Spanish and the waiter understood me perfectly! (He didn't understand Dad's terrible Spanish!)

See you soon.

Alex

3 a Read the tips in the HOW TO box.

b Underline the adjectives Alex uses to describe things.

✔ **Get it right**

Most adjectives come before nouns and after the verb *be*.

*It was a **long flight**.*

*The people **are friendly**.*

PRACTISE

4 Complete each sentence with two of the adjectives in the box.

| amazing | boring | cold | different | fantastic |
| friendly | hot | long | rainy | rude |

1 The journey was _____ / _____ .
2 The food was _____ / _____ .
3 The weather was _____ / _____ .
4 The people were _____ / _____ .
5 I had a(n) _____ / _____ time.

PLAN

5 You're going to write an email message from another country. Use the *Writing plan* to help you prepare.

WRITING PLAN

1 **Say where you are.**
   Which country are you in? Who are you with? How did you get there?

2 **Explain what you did yesterday and this morning.**
   Where did you go? What did you do? What did you see?

3 **Describe things and give your opinion.**
   Look at the tips in the HOW TO box.

WRITE AND CHECK

6 Write your message. Then check it. Tick (✓) the things in the plan.

SHARE

7 Swap your message with other students. Read their messages. Which places would you like to visit?

VOCABULARY Prepositions of movement

1 Complete the information about TinCan with the prepositions in the box.

across	along	around	down	into
out of	past	through	towards	up

TinCan was a cartoon character. In his adventures he travelled (1) .... the world. He also went (2) .... into space in a rocket and (3) .... to the bottom of the sea. He walked (4) .... the Sahara Desert from north to south. In the picture you can see his pet cat Foggy running (5) .... a road. He's running (6) .... some trees (7) .... his master. TinCan often walked (8) .... dangerous situations but he always got (9) .... them before the end of the story. In his most famous adventure, *TinCan in Brazil*, he ran (10) .... the Amazon rainforest.

___ /10

Forms of transport

2 Write the forms of transport TinCan used in his adventures.

1 s_____ p
2 c_____ h
3 h_____ r
4 b____ t
5 m_____ e
6 t____ n
7 p____ e
8 u_____ d
9 l____ y
10 t____ m

___ /10

GRAMMAR Past simple negative

3 Write the verbs in the past simple negative.

TinCan (1) .... (become) a famous character. A lot of people (2) .... (like) him or Foggy the cat. Other people (3) .... (can understand) the stories because they were very complicated. And the drawings (4) .... (look) nice. Stefan Iceberg, the film director, (5) .... (make) a 3-D film version of *TinCan in Brazil* and the artist Horgé (6) .... (win) any prizes.

___ /12

Past simple questions and short answers

4 Write past simple questions and complete the short answers in this conversation between a father and son.

Jordi: you / read / the *TinCan* books when you were young, Dad? (1) ....
Dad: Yes, (2) ....
Jordi: you / like / them? (3) ....
Dad: No, (4) .... They were terrible.
Jordi: you / think / they were funny? (5) ....
Dad: No, (6) .... They were boring.
Jordi: Foggy / be / a nice cat? (7) ....
Dad: No, (8) .... ! He was a horrible cat.
Jordi: Why / you / read them? (9) ....
Dad: I don't know. I can't remember.

___ /18

Your score: ___ /50

SKILLS CHECK

✓✓✓	Yes, I can. No problem!
✓✓	Yes, I can. But I need a bit of help.
✓	Yes, I can. But I need a lot of help.

I can identify the writer's opinion. ....
I can take notes when I listen. ....
I can plan for a night away. ....
I can ask for repetition. ....
I can use descriptive language. ....

READ

1 **Complete the conversation with the phrases (A–H). What does Amir say to Liam?**

EXAM TIPS

match sentences to gaps in a conversation

- Read the conversation with the gaps. What's it about?

- Decide what kind of information is missing. Read the sentences before and after the gap to help you.

- Read the choices. Look for the missing sentences.
  - Read your choice with the sentences before and after it.
  - Does it sound correct? If not, try another sentence.
- You only need to use five of the sentences.

understand new words (2)
See page 78

tell an interesting or funny story
See page 83

Example:

Liam:	Last night I had a strange dream.
Amir:	(0) _____ E _____

Liam:	No you weren't. I was in a room.
Amir:	(1) _____
Liam:	I don't know. It was dark and empty. There was a big mirror at the other end of the room. I walked across and looked into the mirror …
Amir:	(2) _____
Liam:	I saw a baby … and then I saw a child … and the child became a teenager.
Amir:	(3) _____
Liam:	Yes. It was me!
Amir:	(4) _____
Liam:	I grew up and became an adult.
Amir:	(5) _____
Liam:	No, I didn't. I woke up.

A No! You're joking. What happened next?
B That's an amazing story.
C And? What did you see?
D Did you die?
E Was I in the dream?
F Did you recognise him?
G Where was it?
H When were you born?

Reading: _____ /10

LISTEN

2 **3.14** **Listen to Carmel talking to her friend Guy about her holiday. For each question, choose the right answer (A, B or C).**

Example:

0 Who did Carmel stay with?
  A her family
  (B) her pen pal
  C her best friend

---

1 Where does Maya live?
  A Norway   **C** Turkey
  B Japan

2 What's Maya like?
  A shy   **C** friendly
  B serious

3 Maya's grandmother …
  A was very funny.
  B couldn't speak any English.
  C could speak English very well.

4 Before visiting another country, Carmel thinks it's important …
  A to learn some of the language.
  B to find information about it.
  C to take the right clothes.

5 How do you spell 'thank you' in Norwegian?
  A tag   **C** takk
  B tack

Listening: _____ /10

WRITE

3 **Read the information about the club trip and the email. Then write the information in Meggie's notes.**

ADVENTURE CLUB TRIP TO THE LAKE DISTRICT NATIONAL PARK

Next weekend
Coach leaves from outside library at 8.00 on Saturday morning.
Bring warm clothes!

☎ **Phone 775 687 555 for more information.**

From: Sharon	To: Meggie

Hi Meggie! Are you going on the trip to the Lake District? It costs £25. My brother went two years ago. He says it was really amazing. They travelled by train and went swimming every day. I think it's too cold to swim now but we can go on a boat.
Call me tomorrow if you can go. Sharon.

MEGGIE'S NOTES

WHERE?
  Lake District National Park
WHEN?   (1)
TRANSPORT: (2)
HOW MUCH?   (3)
TAKE: (4)
ACTIVITY: (5)

Writing: _____ /10

Progress check score _____ **/30**

UNIT 9 MEET ME AT THE MALL

IN THE PICTURE At the shops

>>> Talk about shops and shopping

WORK WITH WORDS Shops

1 **RECALL** Work in pairs. Make a list of things you can buy at a shopping centre. Add three things to each category. You have two minutes.

Clothes and accessories: _____
Electronic devices: _____
Food: _____
Furniture: _____
Instruments: _____
Pets: _____

2 Match the photos (1–6) to six of the shops in the box.

___ baker's	___ bookshop	___ butcher's	___ chemist
___ clothes shop	___ department store	___ electronics shop	
___ music shop	___ newsagent	___ pet shop	___ sports shop
___ toy shop			

3. Match the definitions (1–6) to the other six shops in the box in Exercise 2.

1 A(n) _____ sells musical instruments.
2 A(n) _____ sells cats, dogs and other animals.
3 A(n) _____ sells magazines and newspapers.
4 A(n) _____ sells medicines, beauty products and toiletries.
5 A(n) _____ sells bread and cakes.
6 A(n) _____ sells meat.

4 ▶3.15 Listen and repeat all the shops in exercises 2 and 3.

5 a ▶3.16 Listen to six conversations. What shops are the people in? Write six different shop names.

b ▶3.16 Listen again and complete what the customer wants.

1 He's looking for _____ .
2 She wants to learn _____ .
3 He wants to buy some _____ and a _____ .
4 She wants to buy a _____ .
5 He's buying some _____ .
6 She needs to buy a _____ , a _____ and a _____ .

✓ **Get it right**
A pet̸s shop sells pets.

6 **THE MOVING PICTURE** ▶ Watch the video. Then work in pairs. How many things can you remember? In what shop (not a department store) can you buy them?

SPEAK

7 Work in pairs. Do the tasks.

1 Think of shops in your town, city or area for each of the adjectives in the box.

big	cheap	cool	expensive
noisy	popular	quiet	small

2 Play the Shop Game. Take it in turns to think of a shop. Your partner has to ask questions to guess its name.

Is it a clothes shop?

Yes, it is.

Is it [name]?

No, it isn't. Try again.

Now it's your turn.

GO BEYOND

Do the Words & Beyond exercise on page 138.

SPEAK AND READ

1 Work in pairs. Answer the questions.

1 Do you like going shopping? Why?/Why not?
2 Where do you normally go shopping?
3 Who do you normally go shopping with?

2 a Read the tips in the HOW TO box.

b Look at the title, photo and first lines of the website article. What's it about? Choose the correct option.

A The favourite shops of the website's readers.
B Where you can buy cheap things.
C How to make good decisions when you go shopping.

3 a Think about the article before you read. Answer the last three questions in the HOW TO box.

b ▶3.17 Now read the article. Next to each tip tick (✓) if you knew this before, and write ! if this is a new idea.

HOW TO

use things you know to help you read

☐ Look at the title, photos and first lines only. What's the text about?

☐ Think about the topic before you read.
 – What do you know about it?
 – What do you expect to read about it?
 – What would you like to know?

HowTo✓

Tips for teens by teens

Thanks everybody for your shopping tips! Here are the top 10.

Shopping: your top 10 tips

Before you go ...
☐ **1 Make a shopping list.** Don't buy other things at the shops.
☐ **2 Do the maths.** How much does everything cost? Only take that much money with you.
☐ **3 Look online first.** Internet shops are often cheaper. Look at prices online before you go shopping.
☐ **4 Find the facts.** Look online for information about things like mobile phones. Know what you need.
☐ **5 Ask Mum or Dad.** Get a parent's opinion about expensive things and not just when they're paying.

At the shops ...
☐ **6 Compare prices.** Some shops are more expensive than others. To save money, compare prices before you buy something.
☐ **7 Don't forget quality.** Compare the quality, not just the price, especially in clothes shops and shoe shops. Sometimes prices are lower but the quality's worse.
☐ **8 Simple is better.** Buy simple clothes. You can wear them when fashions change and make them more interesting with accessories.
☐ **9 Take your time.** If you can't decide, don't spend your money. Leave the shop. A slow decision is better than a bad decision.

Back at home ...
☐ **10 Leave the price on.** When you get home, don't take off the price tag. You can always change things later if you don't like them.

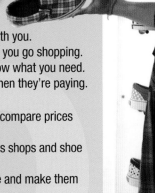

4 Which tips in the HOW TO box helped you understand the text? Tick (✓) them.

5 Read again. Are the sentences right (R) or wrong (W)? If the article doesn't say, write DS.

1 Readers of the website helped with the tips. ....
2 The article's advice is to only buy things online. ....
3 The internet's a good place to find information. ....
4 Parents normally pay for expensive things. ....
5 In general, cheap clothes are bad quality. ....
6 It's good to make a decision quickly in a shop. ....

REACT

6 ⊙ Work in pairs. What did you think of the tips in the article? Compare your opinions.

PHRASE BYTES

I thought the first/second tip was good/bad/interesting ...

What about you?

What did you think of tip number three/four ... ?

GO BEYOND

Read the tips again. Make a list of verbs connected to money and buying things.

READ AND LISTEN >>> Grammar in context

1 ▶3.18 Read and listen to the conversation. Why does Jack really want to go to the shopping centre?

Will: Where are you going, Jack?
Jack: To the shopping centre. I need a new jacket.
Will: What about the local shops?
Jack: They're more expensive than the shopping centre.
Will: Yes, but they're nearer, so you don't have to get a bus. And the service is better.
Tracy: Or what about the second-hand shop? It's cheaper than the shopping centre and the clothes are more original.
Jack: The thing is, Maria's waiting for me at the shopping centre.
Tracy: OK, I understand. See you later!

STUDY

2 Complete the explanations with examples from Exercise 1.

Comparative adjectives

Use: To compare two things.

Form:

short adjective + -er	nearer
more + long adjective	more expensive
irregular adjectives	good > _____
	bad > worse
	far > further

Use *than* after comparatives:
It's cheaper than the shopping centre.
Spelling changes, *big > bigger*, etc: See page 128.
See GRAMMAR DATABASE, page 128.

>>> Workbook, pages 106–107

PRACTISE

3 Complete the sentences with the comparative form of the adjectives. Do you think they're true (*T*) or false (*F*)?

LOCAL SHOPS VS SHOPPING CENTRES
WHAT DO YOU THINK?

1 Shopping centres are *cheaper* (cheap).	T/F
2 People in local shops are _____ (polite).	T/F
3 The service in local shops is _____ (fast).	T/F
4 Shopping centres are _____ (quiet).	T/F
5 Shopping centres are _____ (interesting).	T/F
6 The choice in local shops is _____ (bad).	T/F

4 Complete the sentences about two shops. Use the opposite of the underlined comparative adjective.

1 Trends is <u>older</u> than Wearhouse.
Wearhouse is *newer than* Trends.
2 Wearhouse is <u>smaller</u> than Trends.
Trends is _____ Wearhouse.
3 It's <u>more difficult</u> to find things in Wearhouse.
It's _____ to find things in Trends.
4 Trends is <u>cheaper</u> than Wearhouse.
Wearhouse is _____ Trends.
5 Wearhouse is <u>nearer</u> than Trends.
Trends is _____ Wearhouse.

5 Write sentences giving your opinion. Use the phrases and comparative adjectives.

| 1 | online shopping | popular |
| | real shopping | |

Online shopping is more popular than real shopping. Or: Real shopping is …

| 2 | online shopping | safe |
| | real shopping | |

| 3 | shopping with friends | good |
| | shopping alone | |

| 4 | quality | important |
| | fashion | |

| 5 | older shop assistants | friendly |
| | younger shop assistants | |

| 6 | shopping | interesting |
| | surfing the internet | |

SPEAK

6 Work in pairs. Compare your answers to Exercise 5. Do you agree? If not, why not?

I think …
What do you think?
I agree.
I don't agree.

LISTENING AND VOCABULARY Radio ads

>>> Use important words to help you listen

SPEAK AND LISTEN

1 **Work in pairs. Answer the questions.**

1 How often do you or your family members listen to the radio?
2 Where and when do you (or they) listen to the radio?
3 What do you (or they) listen to – music, the news, adverts … ?

2 a **Read the tips in the HOW TO box.**

b ▶3.19 **Listen to four radio adverts. What's each advert for?**

3 **Which tips in the HOW TO box did you use for help with Exercise 2b? Tick (✓) them.**

4 ▶3.19 **Listen again. Write two answers to each question.**

Advert 1: What can you do at Seaview Plaza?
Advert 2: What can you buy at *The Gear*?
Advert 3: What food is *Molloy's* advertising?
Advert 4: What's good about the Seaview multi-screen complex?

REACT

5 👥 **Work in pairs. Compare the adverts. Which are better? Why?**

WORK WITH WORDS Money and measurements

6 ▶3.20 **Work in pairs. Complete the tables with the words in the box. Then listen and check.**

cent (x2)   dollar   ~~euro~~   kilogram/kilo   kilometre   litre
metre   mile   pence/p   pound (x2)

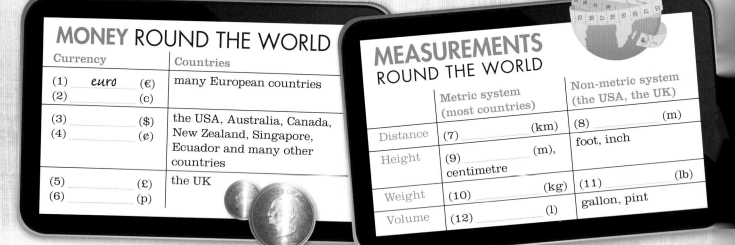

MONEY ROUND THE WORLD

Currency		Countries
(1) *euro*	(€)	many European countries
(2)	(c)	
(3)	($)	the USA, Australia, Canada, New Zealand, Singapore, Ecuador and many other countries
(4)	(¢)	
(5)	(£)	the UK
(6)	(p)	

MEASUREMENTS ROUND THE WORLD

	Metric system (most countries)	Non-metric system (the USA, the UK)
Distance	(7) _____ (km)	(8) _____ (m)
Height	(9) _____ (m), centimetre	foot, inch
Weight	(10) _____ (kg)	(11) _____ (lb)
Volume	(12) _____ (l)	gallon, pint

HOW TO

use important words to help you listen

☐ Listen for the names of people, places and things. They tell you the topic.

☐ Listen for adjectives. They describe things and express opinions.

☐ Listen for verbs. Does the text give general information (present simple) or instructions (imperatives)?

PHRASE BYTES

I liked / didn't like the advert for … because …

Really? I thought it was …

7 a ▶3.21 **Listen and repeat the words in Exercise 6.**

b ▶3.22 **Listen to the short vowel (/ɪ/) in kilogram and the long vowel (/iː/) in kilo. Then listen again and repeat.**

GO BEYOND

Do the Words & Beyond exercise on page 138.

8 ▶3.23 **Listen to two of the adverts in Exercise 2b again. Write the price of these things. Then listen and repeat the prices.**

1 trainers _____
2 tracksuits _____
3 a kilo of potatoes _____
4 two litres of milk _____
5 two chocolate bars _____

9 **Look at the table. Then calculate your weight in pounds and the distance from your house to your school in miles.**

1 kilo = 2.2 pounds	1 mile = 1.6 kilometres

READ >>> Grammar in context

1 Read the advert. What type of shop is MGS Styles?

MGS STYLES

At MGS Styles we have the best selection in town of the coolest fashions. Come to our store to find the most exciting brands at the lowest prices, or visit our website at www.mgsstyles.com.

It has to be MGS STYLES!

STUDY

2 Complete the explanations with examples from Exercise 1.

Superlative adjectives

Use: To compare one thing with all the others in a group.

Form:

the + short adjective + *-est*	*the coolest* _____
the most + long adjective	*the most* _____
irregular adjectives	*good >* _____ *bad > the worst* *far > the furthest*

Spelling changes: See page 128.

See GRAMMAR DATABASE, page 128.

PRACTISE

3 Complete the advert with superlative adjectives.

Fast Fred's

At Fast Fred's we're fast but everything is of the
(1) *highest* (high) quality. We serve the
(2) _____ (tasty) burgers, made of the
(3) _____ (fresh) local ingredients, and we serve them with the (4) _____ (hot),
(5) _____ (health) chips. Our restaurants have the (6) _____ (comfortable) seats!

There's no better place to eat!

Get two meals for the price of one with this advert.

4 Look at the table. Then write sentences about the three mobiles with superlative adjectives.

	CB3.0	M25	R110
1 memory	★★	★★★	★★
2 screen	★★★★	★★	★★★
3 weight	★	★★★★	★★
4 apps	★★★	★★	★★★★
5 price	★★★★	★★	★★★
6 look	★★★	★★★★	★★★

1 _____M25_____ has *the biggest* memory. (big)
2 _____ has _____ screen. (large)
3 _____ is _____ . (heavy)
4 _____ has _____ apps. (amazing)
5 _____ is _____ . (expensive)
6 _____ is _____ phone. (good-looking)

5 Write sentences about your opinions. Use superlative adjectives.

1 cool / shop where I live
   The coolest shop where I live is …
2 funny / advert on TV
3 dangerous / sport
4 bad / food
5 boring / activity at the weekend
6 good / film of all time

6 a ▶3.24 **PRONOUNCE** Listen to the vowel sound in *worse* /ɜː/.

b ▶3.25 Listen and repeat the sentences. Pronounce the underlined /ɜː/ sound.

The worst shirt in the world.
The first word I heard.

SPEAK

7 Work in groups. Compare your opinions in Exercise 5. Choose the best opinion for each thing (1–6). Then tell other groups. Do they agree?

What did you write for number … ?

I wrote … . What about you?

So which opinion is the best?

I think …

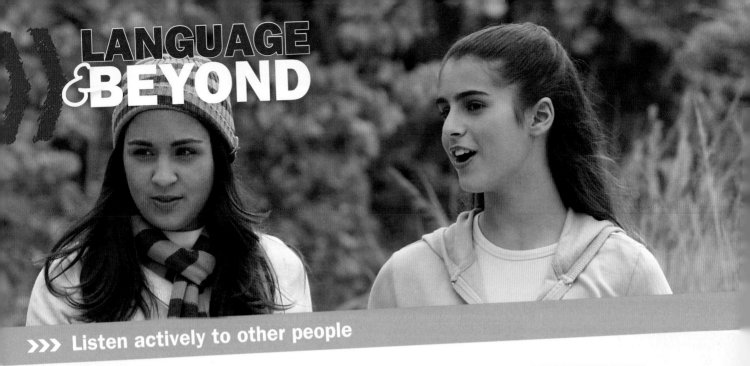

LANGUAGE &BEYOND

>>> Listen actively to other people

SPEAK AND WRITE

1 **Work in groups. Talk about the last time you went shopping.**

2 **Make a note of what other people said in Exercise 1. Then choose the best option (A–D) to describe what you did.**
   A I listened actively and remembered what the others said.
   B I listened but also planned what I wanted to say.
   C I tried to listen but it was hard. I didn't remember much.
   D I didn't listen much because I wanted to talk.

3 **Why is it important to listen actively? Choose the most important reason. Then compare your answer with other students.**
   A It shows you respect them.
   B You can learn things from them.
   C You hear different opinions.
   D It's a good way to make friends.

DO

4 **Tick (✓) the statements that you agree with.**

Fashion
'I follow fashion. It's really important to me.'
'Fashion's OK but it's better to be different.'
'Fashion's just a way for shops to make more money.'

Brands
'Brands are more expensive but the clothes are better quality.'
'When you buy brands, you pay more for the name.'
'Brands are important. They help you feel part of a group.'

5 **Work in groups. Discuss brands OR fashion. Listen actively. Then answer the questions about your discussion.**
   1 Did everybody speak? If not, why not?
   2 What did most people think about fashion or brands?

REFLECT

6 **Talk about the questions. Then read the** REFLECTION POINT **.**
   1 Why can it sometimes be difficult to listen actively to other people?
   2 What did you think was the most important reason for listening actively to others? Explain why.
   3 Will you listen more actively to people in future? Why?/Why not?

EXTEND

7 **Work in groups. Discuss the other topic in Exercise 5. Try to listen actively during the discussion.**

When did you last go shopping?

Where did you go?

What did you buy?

Who did you go with?

PHRASE BYTES

What reason did you choose?

I think the most important reason is that …

Me too.

Really? I chose that …

REFLECTION POINT

Sometimes it's difficult to *really* listen to others but it's important. It shows you respect them. It's also a good way to learn new things and understand how other people see the world.

RESPECT OTHERS

>>> Workbook, page 113

SPEAK

1 **Work in pairs. Answer the questions.**

1 Where's the nearest market to your home?
2 How often do you buy things at a market? What things?

WATCH OR LISTEN

2 ▶ 3.26 **Watch or listen to the scenes. What does Alex buy at the market? How much does he spend?**

1
May: Who's next, please?
Alex: I am. (1) .... some apples.
May: Which **ones**?
Alex: Those red **ones** over there. (2) .... they?
May: £1.60 a kilo.
Alex: Sorry, did you say £1.60?
May: That's right.
Alex: (3) .... a kilo, please?

2
Ryan: Can I help you?
Alex: Yes. (4) .... a cheese and tomato sandwich, please?
Ryan: Would you like a white or a granary roll?
Alex: Sorry, could you repeat that?
Ryan: Would you like a white or a granary roll?
Alex: Granary? Does that mean brown?
Ryan: Yeah. It's this **one**.
Alex: (5) .... a granary roll, then, please. And an orange juice. (6) .... that?
Ryan: That's £5.20.

3 ▶ 3.26 **Watch or listen again and complete the conversations.**

4 **a** **Read the tips in the HOW TO box.**

b **Find three examples of checking that you understand in the conversations.**

5 **We can use *one* and *ones* in place of nouns. What do *one* and *ones* in bold in Exercise 2 refer to?**

6 ▶ 3.27 **Listen and repeat the sentences from the conversations.**

HOW TO ?

check that you understand

■ Ask the other person a question:
– Sorry, did you say … ?
– Does that mean … ?
– Do you mean … ?

■ If necessary, ask for repetition:
– Sorry, can/could you repeat that, please?

ACT

7 **a** ◯ **Work in pairs. Prepare a conversation at a market. One of you wants to buy food or clothes, the other is selling those things. Include prices and phrases for checking that you understand.**

b **Present your conversation to other students. For other conversations, write what the customer buys and the prices.**

PHRASEBOOK ▶ 3.28

Buy things	Check that you understand
I'd like …	Sorry, did you say … ?
Would you like … ?	Sorry, can/could you repeat that?
Can I have … ?	
Which one/ones?	Does that mean … ?
The/That red/big one.	Do you mean … ?
The/Those blue/old ones.	
How much is/are … ?	

SPEAK AND READ

1 **Work in pairs. Read the advert and answer the questions.**

  1 Do you think it's a good advert? Why?/Why not?

  2 Where do you see adverts like this?

  3 Do you ever buy things after you see an advert?

EVERYDAY ELECTRONICS

Come to Everyday Electronics, the <u>bigest</u> and best electronics shop in town! We have all the latest gadgets – the coolest mobiles, the fastest tablets, the most amazing video games. We also have <u>beter</u> prices than any other shop in <u>england</u> and the <u>friendlyest</u>, most helpful sales <u>peoples</u>.

At Everyday Electronics your money <u>gos</u> further! That's why a million customers <u>shoped</u> in our stores last year.

Everyday Electronics – now in more than 50 <u>citys</u>!

2 **a** **Read the tips in the `HOW TO` box.**

  b **Correct the <u>underlined</u> mistakes in the advert.**

PRACTISE

3 **Find and correct 10 mistakes in the advert.**

BARGAIN BOOKS

we have the largeest selection of new and second-hand books in london find the latest literature in english and books and magazines from over 100 diferent countrys. Or look at our used book shelf for our best posible prices.

Bargain Books dos more to make you read.

> **HOW TO**
>
> check your writing
>
> - Check your spelling.
>   - Spelling sometimes changes when you add -s, -er/est, -ing or -ed.
>   - Some plurals and comparatives/superlatives are irregular.
>   - Use a dictionary or computer spellchecker.
> - Check your punctuation (see page 18).

PLAN

4 **You're going to write an advert for a shop. Use the *Writing plan* to help you prepare.**

WRITING PLAN

  1 **Choose a shop.**

    What type of shop do you want to advertise?

  2 **Think about how to advertise it.**

    Why is it special? Why is it better than other shops?

  3 **Compare it with other shops.**

    Use comparative and superlative adjectives.

  4 **Check your advert when you finish.**

    Look at the tips in the `HOW TO` box.

WRITE AND CHECK

5 **Write your advert. Then check it. Tick (✓) the things in the plan.**

SHARE

6 **Swap your advert with other students. Which shops do you most want to visit?**

VOCABULARY Shops

1 Complete the shops.

> **Welcome to the Online MultiStore! Click on a link to go to one of our shops.**

(1) b _____'s *bread, cakes*
(2) b _____ *novels, comics*
(3) bu _____'s *meat, chicken*
(4) ch _____ *medicine, sun cream*
(5) cl _____ shop *jeans, T-shirts*
(6) el _____ shop
mobiles, tablets
(7) m _____ shop *guitars, pianos*
(8) new _____ *magazines, pens*
(9) p _____ shop *cats, birds*
(10) s _____ shop *rackets, boots*
(11) t _____ shop *games, puzzles*
The Online MultiStore is the web's biggest
(12) dep _____
st _____ .   ___/12

Money and measurements

2 Complete the instructions with the words in the box.

> cent (x2)   dollar   euro   kilo   kilometre
> litre   metre   mile   pence   pound (x2)

> ## Online MultiStore!
>
> | Home | Country | About | Log in |
>
> Click on <u>EU</u> for our European store
> Prices are in (1) _____ s and (2) _____ s.
> Weights are in (3) _____ s and volumes in
> (4) _____ s.
> Product sizes are in centimetres and (5) _____ s
> and delivery distances are in (6) _____ s.
> Click on <u>US</u> for our American store
> Prices are in (7) _____ s and (8) _____ s.
> Weights are in (9) _____ s and delivery
> distances are in (10) _____ s.
> Click on <u>UK</u> for our British store
> Prices are in (11) _____ s and
> (12) _____ .   ___/12

GRAMMAR Comparative adjectives

3 Complete the advert with the comparative form of the adjectives.

> **Why shop at the Online MultiStore?**
>
> We're (1) _____ (cheap) than other
> stores.
> We have a (2) _____ (big) selection of
> products.
> Our delivery service is (3) _____ (fast).
> We send things (4) _____ (far) than
> other online stores.
> Our website is (5) _____ (easy) to use.
> Our phone operators are (6) _____
> (cheerful).
> We're simply (7) _____ (good)
> than the rest!   ___/14

Superlative adjectives

4 Complete the customer opinions with the superlative form of the adjectives.

> ★★★★ The Online MultiStore has
> (1) _____ (amazing) offers you can find
> online!
> ★★★ They have (2) _____ (fast) website
> of any online store.
> ★★★ Definitely (3) _____ (friendly)
> phone operators on the web!
> ★★ It isn't (4) _____ (expensive) store on
> the Net but it isn't cheap.
> ★ Their phone operators are (5) _____
> (rude) people in the business!
> ★ This is (6) _____ (bad)
> store on the web.   ___/12
>
> Your score: ___/50

SKILLS CHECK

✓✓✓ Yes, I can. No problem!	
✓✓ Yes, I can. But I need a bit of help.	
✓ Yes, I can. But I need a lot of help.	

I can use things I know to help me read. _____
I can use important words to help me listen. _____
I can listen actively to other people. _____
I can buy things at a market. _____
I can check my writing. _____

UNIT **10** **SPECIAL DAYS**

IN THE PICTURE A world of festivals

>>> **Talk about festivals and celebrations**

a
October/November

WORK WITH WORDS Festivals

1 (RECALL) **Write the words in the box next to the correct verbs.**

a party   a special meal   presents   the drums   the guitar

give/get (1) _____
have (2) _____ / (3) _____
play (4) _____ / (5) _____

2 a **Work in pairs. Match the festivals (1–5) to the photos (a–e).**

1 Chinese New Year
2 Diwali, Festival of Lights
3 Maslenitsa, Russian festival
4 Notting Hill Carnival
5 St Patrick's Day

b ▶3.29 **Listen and check. What city has all the festivals?**

3 a ▶3.29 **Read the sentences. Then listen again. Circle the photos or the things in the photos for the words in bold.**

1 Maslenitsa is a Russian **celebration**.
2 People are wearing amazing **costumes**.
3 There are red **decorations** everywhere.
4 We can hear and see some **fireworks**.
5 It's beautiful here with all the lights and **candles**.
6 Hundreds of people are walking along the street in the **parade**.

b **Write the correct photo for the sentences.**

1 **Invite** all your friends to come and eat Caribbean food.
2 **Wish** everyone a Happy New Year.
3 **Celebrate** with South Asian music.
4 **Decorate** your face with green paint.

c ▶3.30 **Listen. Repeat all the words in bold in exercises 3a and 3b.**

4 a ▶3.31 (PRONOUNCE) **Listen to the /ʃ/ sounds and repeat.**

celebration   decoration

b ▶3.32 **Listen and repeat. Pay attention to the /ʃ/ sound.**

spe**ci**al   Ru**ss**ian   Iri**sh**   **sh**ow   atten**ti**on

5 **Complete the speech bubbles (1–6) with the correct words from exercises 3a and 3b.**

1 I'm happy we could _____ Diwali together.

2 I don't like _____ s – they're too noisy. Our dog hates them too.

3 I _____ you lots of luck.

4 I love your _____ and hat.

5 Did you _____ Jaya to the festival?

6 Let's make New Year _____ s for our flat.

Festivals Calendar

January	February	March	April	May	June
July	August	September	October	November	December

b

February/March

c

March

IRISH
GREENW

e

January

d

August

---

6 **THE MOVING PICTURE** ▶ Watch the video. Which things from Exercise 3a can you see? Which festival would you most like to go to? Why?

SPEAK

7 Tell a partner about a festival you know. Remember these things:

- the date or time of year
- costumes
- music and dancing
- decorations
- food
- special activities

PHRASE BYTES

I want to tell you about …

It's a festival in …

People wear/eat …

GO BEYOND

Do the Words & Beyond exercise on page 139.

>>> **Make notes when you read**

SPEAK AND READ

1 **Work in pairs. Look at the website. In what part of the UK is Cornwall – north, south, east or west? Check on a map or map app to see if you were right.**

Golowan Festival

Home   About   Schedule   Blog

Golowan **means 'midsummer' in Cornish, the old language of Cornwall. Midsummer is the longest day of the year and people celebrate it in many countries. In the past people celebrated Golowan in Penzance with large bonfires and other activities with fire. But the town stopped the festival as people thought it was too dangerous.**

People from Penzance started the festival again in 1990. Now the celebration lasts for 10 days – and it's very safe! Everyone comes from the town and visitors come from other parts of Cornwall. This year on 'Mazey Eve', the night before the most important day, there's going to be a big fireworks show and lots of different music events. The main day is 'Mazey Day'. On that day cars and buses can't use the roads in the town centre and people decorate the streets with flags in different colours. Penzance school students make their own costumes.

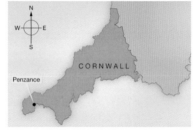

They also make amazing people and animals out of paper. This year the theme is 'giants'. Students and their teachers are going to carry their giants in a parade through the streets of the town. People are also going to play music in the streets, tell stories and sell Cornish food, clothes and presents.

Search

Subscribe

Dates for your diary

Mazey Eve: 28th June, by the sea
Mazey Day: 29th June, town centre

2 a **Read the tips in the HOW TO box.**

b (▶3.33) **Your school is planning a trip to Cornwall for the end of the school year. Read the website information and make notes for your parents. Use the tips in the HOW TO box to help you.**

3 **Which tips in the HOW TO box did you use for help with Exercise 2b? Tick (✓) them.**

4 🗣 **Work in pairs. Your partner is your parent. Tell him/her about the festival. Use your notes from Exercise 2b.**

REACT

5 **Work in pairs. Answer the questions.**
1 What months are summer months in your country?
2 Are there any special celebrations in the summer in your country? What happens?
3 What is the best thing about summer for you?

HOW TO

make notes when you read

☐ Decide what information you need (*What? Where? When? Why?*).

☐ Read the text and underline or highlight important information (names, places, dates, explanations).

☐ Only write important words or phrases.

PHRASE BYTES

There's a school trip to …

There's a festival in …

It's to celebrate …

People make/carry …

It's on …

GO BEYOND

Write a short advert for Mazey Day. Think of: *What? Where?* and *When?*

READ AND LISTEN >>> Grammar in context

1 ▶**3.34** **Read and listen to the conversation. Who's planning to go to the parade?**

Malik: We're going to watch the St Patrick's Day parade tomorrow. Are you going to be there?

Lucy: No, I'm not. My mum's going to be at work.

Malik: You can come with me and my parents. My sister isn't going to come, so there's space in the car.

Lucy: OK – thanks! What time are you going to leave your house?

Malik: At 10 o'clock. We aren't going to stay for the concert because I'm going to watch football in the evening.

Lucy: That's fine. I need to practise playing my guitar tomorrow too.

STUDY

2 a **Read the explanations. Complete the examples from Exercise 1.**

Going to
Use: For plans in the future.
Form:
Positive
I am / You are / He is, etc *going to* + verb
We _____ the parade.
Negative
I'm not / You aren't / He isn't, etc *going to* + verb
My sister _____ .
Questions and short answers
Am/Are/Is + I/you/she, etc + *going to* + verb
_____ *there?*
Yes, I am. / No, _____ .
See GRAMMAR DATABASE, page 129.

b **Underline three different time expressions in Exercise 1.**

PRACTISE

3 **Complete the announcement with the correct words.**

'Hello everybody! The parade (1) ___is___ going to start in two minutes. It's going to (2) _____ our best parade ever and we're going (3) _____ have a great time! A lot of people (4) _____ going to walk along the streets, so please keep back. Now I (5) _____ going to count down to zero and you're (6) _____ to help me! Ten, nine …'

4 **Malik and Lucy are having a great time. Write sentences with the negative form of *going to*.**

1 Malik's parents / not drive / back / early.
Malik's parents aren't going to drive back early.

2 Malik and Lucy / not go home / now.

3 **Malik:** 'I / not watch / football.'

4 Lucy / not practise / guitar.

5 **Lucy:** 'We / not miss / the big concert.'

5 **Malik and Lucy met some friends. Put the words in order to make questions. Then choose the correct answer.**

Malik: (1) going to / What / you / tomorrow / are / do?
What are you going to do tomorrow?

Scott: **A** No, I'm not.
Ⓑ I'm not going to do anything special.

Flora: (2) at home / your mum / Is / be / on Sunday / going to?

Lucy: **A** Yes, she is. **B** Yes, she isn't going to get home until late at night.

Lucy: (3) drive / going to / next Saturday / your parents / to the beach / Are / you?

Scott: **A** No, we aren't. **B** Yes, and then they're going to visit my grandma.

Malik: (4) I / come / to your house / Am / tomorrow / going to?

Flora: **A** No, I'm going to come to *your* house. **B** Yes, we are.

SPEAK

6 a **Make questions with *going to* for your partner. Use a question word if necessary.**

1 do sport after school?
Are you going to do sport after school?

2 do this evening?
What …

3 stay at home tomorrow?

4 get up on Saturday?

5 go at the weekend?

b **Work in pairs. Ask and answer the questions.**

Are you going to do sport after school?

Yes, I am. I'm going to play tennis.

No, I'm not. I'm going to go home.

LISTENING AND VOCABULARY World days

WORK WITH WORDS Feelings

1 Work in pairs. Answer the questions.

1. How often do you use emoticons like the ones below? When?
2. What emoticons do you normally see for these adjectives? Draw them.

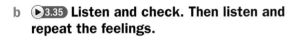

cool   funny   happy   sad   tired

2 a Work in pairs. Match the emoticons (1–10) to the feelings in the box.

8 afraid	angry	bored	embarrassed
excited	interested	nervous	
relaxed	surprised	worried	

b ▶3.35 Listen and check. Then listen and repeat the feelings.

3 a How do people often feel in these situations? Write an adjective from Exercise 2a.

1. when it's their birthday
2. when somebody reads their diary
3. when their exam results are better than usual
4. if they fall asleep in class
5. when they sit in the sun
6. before an important exam
7. when they forget their homework
8. when they talk about their hobby
9. on a long car or train journey
10. when they see a big spider

b Work in pairs. Compare your answers. Then decide which feelings are positive and which are negative.

LISTEN AND SPEAK

4 ▶3.36 Listen to some radio interviews in the street and answer the questions.

1. What's the interview about?
2. How many people does the presenter talk to?
3. What special day does the last speaker mention?

5 a Read the tips in the **HOW TO** box.

b ▶3.36 Listen again. Circle if the person's feelings are positive (*P*) or negative (*N*). If they change, circle *C*.

Anika: P/N/C
Kari: P/N/C
Mark: P/N/C
Nasir: P/N/C

6 Which tips in the **HOW TO** box did you use for help with Exercise 5b? Tick (✓) them.

REACT

7 Work in pairs. Answer the questions.

1. Do you want to celebrate International Talk Like A Pirate Day? Why?/Why not?
2. Say 'Ahoy there!' like a pirate. How do you feel?

PHRASE BYTES

I hardly ever / never use emoticons.

I sometimes/often use emoticons when …

The happy emoticon's like this.

Ahoy there!

PHRASE BYTES

What's your answer for … ?

I've got the same answer.

Really? I feel … when …

I think being … is positive/ negative.

HOW TO

identify positive and negative feelings

☐ Listen to <u>what</u> speakers say:
 – Do they say how they feel?
 – Do they use positive or negative adjectives?

☐ Listen to <u>how</u> they speak. Do they sound happy or not?

PHRASE BYTES

I want / don't want to …

I think it's fun/stupid …

I feel a little/really …

GO BEYOND

Do the Words & Beyond exercise on page 139.

>>> Predict things in the future

READ AND LISTEN >>> Grammar in context

1 ▶3.37 **Read and listen to the conversation. What's today's class about?**

Teacher: Will your dinner be ready when you get home this evening? Sean? Moya?

Sean: Yes, it will. I'm hungry now!

Moya: No, it won't. We eat late on Wednesdays.

Teacher: OK. But you'll have dinner.

Moya: Of course!

Teacher: Because a lot of people round the world won't eat tonight. And many people think the price of food will be a problem for everybody in the future. That's why World Food Day is so important. And that's the subject of today's lesson.

STUDY

2 **Complete the examples from Exercise 1.**

Will for predictions

Use: For predictions about the future.

Form:

Positive and negative

I/you/he, etc + *will/won't* + verb

will > 'll will not > won't

The price of food _____ *a problem.*

But _____ *dinner.*

A lot of people _____ *tonight.*

Questions and short answers

Will + I/you/she, etc + verb _____ *ready?*

Yes, I/you/it will. / No, I/you/it won't.

Note:

Use *think* or *don't think* + *will* if you're not sure:

She thinks we'll have enough food.

See GRAMMAR DATABASE, page 129.

>>> Workbook, page 122

PRACTISE

3 ▶3.38 **Complete the conversation with *will* and short answers. Then listen and check.**

Avril: We talked about International Mother Language Day in class. It was really interesting. The teacher thinks a lot of languages (1) _____ (die) out. People (2) _____ (not use) them.

Moya: Why's that?

Avril: Because everybody (3) _____ (speak) Spanish, Chinese or English.

Moya: What about Irish? (4) _____ (people / speak) Irish in the future?

Avril: Yes, they (5) _____ . We (6) _____ (continue) to learn Irish at school, so it (7) _____ (survive). But other languages (8) _____ (not be) so lucky. That's why International Mother Language Day is so important.

4 a **Make the predictions true for you with *will* or *won't*.**

1 People _____ speak my mother language 50 years from now.
2 My country _____ win the next football World Cup.
3 I _____ have the same classmates next year.
4 Next week _____ be a good week for me.
5 My dinner _____ be ready when I get home tonight.
6 The teacher _____ give us a lot of homework today.

b **Compare your predictions with other students. Are they the same or different?**

WRITE AND SPEAK

5 a **Work in pairs. First, write predictions about your partner with *will* and *won't*. If you're not sure, use *I think / don't think* with *will*.**

1 speak / English at the weekend.
2 be / late for school tomorrow.
3 have / a big 18th birthday party.
4 spend / New Year's Eve with his/her family.
5 feel / bored on Sunday evening.
6 get / good marks in the next English test.

b **Write questions for your partner with *will* to check your predictions. Then ask your questions.**

Will you speak English at the weekend?

Yes, I will.

No, I won't.

No, I don't think I will.

LANGUAGE & BEYOND

Speech bubble (Lidia): "Sandra, I invited 14 people to my birthday and only eight are here. And look at all that extra food!"

Speech bubble (Sandra): "OK, six people aren't here. But you sent the invitations late, Lidia. Your best friends are here and we're having a great time. You can eat the extra food tomorrow."

>>> See things in a positive way

KNOW YOURSELF

SPEAK AND READ

1 a Work in pairs. Describe the picture. How do the people feel?

b Read the conversation. Then answer the questions.

1 How do Lidia and Sandra feel?
2 Who sees things in a positive way?

DO

2 Work in pairs. Look at the tips and answer the questions.

1 Do you think they're good tips? Why?/Why not?
2 Which tips does Sandra use when she talks to Lidia?

3 Work in groups. How can Ron, Sima and Jordi see their situation in a positive way? Use the tips in Exercise 2.

Ron: 'We're going to live in another city. I'm worried because I won't know anybody and I won't see my friends here again.'

Sima: 'There was a concert at school and I played the guitar. It was terrible! I felt very nervous and made lots of mistakes.'

Jordi: 'I needed a new mobile and my parents gave me one for my birthday. But I'm angry because it wasn't the one I wanted.'

REFLECT

4 Talk about the questions. Then read the **REFLECTION POINT**.

1 Is it easy or hard for Ron, Sima and Jordi to be positive? Why?
2 Why is it better to think about things in a positive way?
3 Can everybody learn to be more positive? Why?/Why not?

EXTEND

5 a Think about a time when you had negative feelings about a situation. Try to think of a positive way to see the same situation.

b Tell a partner about the situation and your feelings now.

TIPS FOR LIFE
HOW TO BE POSITIVE!

1 Think about the good things in a situation, not the bad things.
2 Don't worry about problems. Find a solution. Most problems have a solution.
3 Don't be afraid of mistakes. They teach you to do things better.

PHRASE BYTES

Ron's situation is positive because …

That's right. And his friends will write/send …

Sima made mistakes but she'll …

Jordi's unhappy but …

REFLECTION POINT «

When you first look at a situation, it's easy to see the bad things. But you can always find a positive way to see things. You can always learn positive things from your mistakes too.

>>> **Give wishes and congratulate people**

SPEAK

1 **You congratulate people or give them your best wishes when it's a special day, or when they do something difficult. Work in pairs. Think of three situations when you congratulate people.**

WATCH OR LISTEN

2 **▶▶3.39 Watch or listen to the scene. Does it include your situations in Exercise 1?**

Adam:	It's Joe's birthday today.
Skye:	That's right. Let's phone him.
Adam:	Joe? Hi. I'm with Skye and Rose. Just a moment …
All:	Happy birthday!
Luca:	What's going on?
Adam:	It's Joe's birthday.
Luca:	(1) _____ him a happy birthday from me.
Adam:	Luca (2) _____ you a happy birthday too. … How did the piano exam go? … Wow! Congratulations! Good luck with your audition. … Don't worry, you'll be fine.
Skye:	Good luck!
Rose:	Yeah, good luck, Joe!
Adam:	Did you hear that? … He says thanks. So what are your plans? … Cool. Well, (3) _____ a good day! … OK, (4) _____ the concert. … OK, bye for now. Bye.

3 **▶▶3.39 Watch or listen again and complete the conversation with three different verbs.**

4 **Work in pairs. Complete the sentences with the phrases in the box. Sometimes there is more than one phrase for a sentence.**

> a good time   a good week   in your new school   New Year
> with your project   your holiday   your meal

1 Happy _____ .   3 Enjoy _____ .
2 Have _____ .   4 Good luck _____ .

5 **What do you say? Write Congratulations! (C) or Good luck! (GL) next to the situations.**

1 A friend has an important match tomorrow.
2 A friend won first prize in a talent show.
3 Your aunt recently had a baby.
4 Your mother/father is going to have a job interview.

6 **▶3.40 Listen and repeat the expressions.**

ACT

7 a ⊕ **Work in pairs. Prepare and practise a conversation with a friend. Use the ideas below and the** PHRASEBOOK **expressions.**

> It's his/her birthday.
> He/She's got an English exam tomorrow.
> He/She won first prize in a drawing competition.
> He/She's going to a party on Saturday.
> He/She's in a new play on Friday night.
> He/She's going to the beach at the weekend.

b **Present your conversation to another pair.**

PHRASEBOOK ▶3.41

Give wishes
Happy birthday / New Year …
Wish him/her a happy … from me.
Good luck!
Good luck with/in …
Have a good …
Enjoy the/your …

Congratulate people
Congratulations!

WRITING Let's celebrate!

>>> Use typical phrases in invitations

SPEAK AND READ

1 Work in pairs. Answer the questions.

1 What special days do you celebrate in your family?
2 What do you do to celebrate your birthday?
3 Does your school have parties for students? What kind of parties?

2 Read the two invitations. What kinds of parties are they?

3 a Read the tips in the HOW TO box.

HOW TO

use typical phrases in invitations

- Use these phrases for headings: *Let's celebrate!*, *Let's party!*
- Use these phrases to invite people: *I'd like to invite you to … , Please come to … , Please join us/me for … , Come and celebrate … .*
- Use *Dress code* for special clothes or costumes.
- Use *RSVP by …* to ask for replies to the invitation.

b Find some of the phrases in the HOW TO box in the invitations. How do the phrases finish?

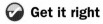 **Get it right**

Use the 12-hour clock with *am* and *pm,* or the 24-hour clock without *am* and *pm*.

PRACTISE

4 Replace the underlined words with a phrase from Exercise 3a.

1 <u>Please tell me if you can come</u> by August 1st.
2 <u>I want to give you an invitation</u> to my party.
3 <u>We want you to wear these clothes</u>: 80s fashion.
4 <u>We want you to be at</u> our party.

PLAN

5 You're going to write an invitation to a party. First, decide what kind of party it is. Use the *Writing plan* to help you prepare.

WRITING PLAN

1 **Use a heading for your invitation.**

2 **Write the main information about the party.**
   What's the party for? When is it? What time? Where is it?

2 **Write other details.**
   Is there a dress code? Are there tickets? What are you going to do?

3 **Ask for replies.**
   Give a date and phone number or email address.

WRITE AND CHECK

6 Write your invitation. Then check it. Tick (✓) the things in the plan.

SHARE

7 Swap your invitation with other students. Read their invitations. Which parties would you like to go to? Why?

VOCABULARY Festivals

1 The students in Lynn's class are organising a party. Complete her notes with the words in the box.

candle   celebrate   celebration   costume   decorate
decorations   fireworks   invite   parade   wish

Meeting to organise end-of-year (1) _____
What's the best way to (2) _____ the end of the school year and (3) _____ everyone a happy summer?
- A (4) _____ in the street?
  No – difficult to organise and get permission.
- (5) _____ ?
  No – noisy, expensive and dangerous.
- Film stars party with a prize for the best
  (6) _____ ?
  Yes! We can (7) _____ our classroom and put
  (8) _____ around the school too. We can also make a
  cupcake with a (9) _____ for every student. _____
- Do we (10) _____ other classes?
  No – better if it's just us!   ___ /10

Feelings

2 Complete the feelings in part of Lynn's email about the meeting.

✉ New mail   ← Reply   ➡ Forward   ✖

I was (1) wo_____ before the meeting because there are often problems. But most people were calm and (2) re_____.
Greg was (3) an_____ because we didn't ask for his opinion. Monica felt (4) em_____ because people laughed at her idea. Tim was (5) bo_____ and played with his phone. And Kevin said he wants to play the guitar but he's (6) ne_____ because he's (7) af_____ to make mistakes. But we're (8) ex_____ and can't wait for the party. The teacher's (9) in_____ too. She's asking lots of questions. And she's (10) su_____ because we organised everything with no help. _____

                                               ___ /10

GRAMMAR Going to

3 Complete the conversation with the correct form of *going to* and short answers.

Teacher: Lynn, (1) _____ (you / have) another meeting about the party?
Lynn: No, we (2) _____ . We (3) _____ (prepare) things in small groups.
Teacher: Great. (4) _____ (Lewis / make) the cake?
Lynn: Yes, he (5) _____ .
Teacher: That's good! What type of cake (6) _____ (he / make)?
Lynn: He (7) _____ (not tell) us. It (8) _____ (be) a surprise.
Teacher: Well, let me know if you need anything.

                                               ___ /16

Will for predictions

4 Complete the conversation with the correct form of *will* and short answers.

Monica: Lynn, (1) _____ (the party / be) OK?
Lynn: Yes, (2) _____ . I think it (3) _____ (go) really well. Why do you ask?
Monica: Well, it's a holiday next week, so we (4) _____ (not have) much time to prepare things. (5) _____ (there / be) time to organise the music, for example?
Lynn: Organising the music (6) _____ (not take) long. But we (7) _____ (need) to have another meeting!

                                               ___ /14

                                 Your score: ___ /50

SKILLS CHECK

✓✓✓ Yes, I can. No problem!
✓✓   Yes, I can. But I need a bit of help.
✓   Yes, I can. But I need a lot of help.

I can make notes when I read.   _____
I can identify positive and negative feelings when I listen.   _____
I can see things in a positive way.   _____
I can give wishes and congratulate people.   _____
I can use typical phrases in invitations.   _____

READ

1 **Read the information from a guidebook about the markets of Marrakech, Morocco. Choose the best word (A, B or C) for each space.**

Example:

0	**A**	want	**(B)**	going		**C**	planned

1	**A**	make	**B**	have		**C**	go
2	**A**	smallest	**B**	biggest		**C**	newest
3	**A**	most	**B**	much		**C**	more
4	**A**	miles	**B**	kilos		**C**	grams
5	**A**	money	**B**	distance		**C**	price
6	**A**	pounds	**B**	pence		**C**	dollars
7	**A**	that	**B**	than		**C**	because
8	**A**	always	**B**	never		**C**	not
9	**A**	will	**B**	won't		**C**	don't
10	**A**	on	**B**	to		**C**	and

Reading: _____ /10

EXAM TIPS

complete gaps in a text with multiple choice answers

- Quickly read the text. What's it about?

- Look at the example. It shows you what to do.

- Read each sentence. Do you have an idea for the gap?

- Look at the choices. Is your idea there? If not, choose the best word.

- Read the text with your answers to check it.

use things you know to help you read
See page 100

THE MARKETS OF MARRAKECH

If you're (0) *going* to visit Marrakech, (1) _____ shopping at the *souks*, the traditional old markets. The Marrakech souks are the (2) _____ markets in Morocco – there are 18 different ones together. They're also some of the (3) _____ amazing markets in the world. There are (4) _____ of spices, and beautiful carpets, clothes and shoes. Sellers can often tell you the (5) _____ in euros and American (6) _____ in different languages. A lot of things are cheaper (7) _____ in other countries but don't pay the seller's first price: you should (8) _____ offer half and then agree on a price. Remember: you (9) _____ need an extra bag for all your souvenirs!
Open from 9am (10) _____ 9pm.

LISTEN

2 3.42 **You will hear a recorded phone message. Listen and complete the notes.**

Crossington Shopping Centre
Opening times Monday–Thursday: _9am–7pm_
Opening times Friday–Saturday: **(1)** _____
Crossington's 20th birthday celebrations
Start Friday 15th: concert with **(2)** _____
Saturday: **(3)** Teen Fashion Day
(_____ of models)
Activities: **(4)** make _____ and candles
For more information, phone: **(5)** _____

Listening: _____ /10

WRITE

3 **Read the descriptions and complete the words for feelings.**

0 People feel like this when they're on holiday.
_r e l a x e d_
1 Some people feel like this before a test or presentation.
n _____
2 Some people go red in the face when they feel like this.
e _____
3 People feel like this when nothing interesting is happening.
b _____
4 People usually feel like this in a dangerous situation.
a _____
5 People feel like this when somebody does something bad.
a _____

_____ /5

4 **Read the message from your friend Emma. Write a reply. Send Emma an invitation to your party with the information she wants. (25–35 words)**

_____ 5 minutes ago ✉
Are you going to have a party for your birthday again this year?
What date is it and what time does it start? What are we going
to do? Do we have to wear costumes like last year?
_____ Comment Like

_____ /5

Writing: _____ /10

Progress check score _____ /30

⟫⟫⟫ Download extra speaking activities from www.macmillanbeyond.com

There is / there are

USE

- Use *there is / there are* to describe what's in a place:
  *In my town **there's** a big park.*
  ***There isn't** a cinema or a zoo.*
  ***There are** lots of shops.*

FORM

Positive

***There's** a restaurant.*
***There are** some cafés.*

- *There's* is the short form of *there is.* You usually use the short form in informal spoken and written English.
- You often use *some* with *there are* and plural nouns.

Negative

***There isn't** a swimming pool.*
***There aren't** any tall buildings.*

- You often use *any* with *there aren't* and plural nouns.
- *There isn't* and *there aren't* are the short forms of *there is not* and *there are not.* You usually use the short forms in informal spoken and written English.

Questions and short answers

***Is there** a shopping centre?*	*Yes, **there is.** / No, **there isn't.***
***Are there** any sports clubs?*	*Yes, **there are.** / No, **there aren't.***

Have got

USE

- Use *have got* to talk about relationships and possessions:
  *I've **got** one brother.*
  *I **haven't got** any sisters.*
  *My brother's **got** brown hair.*

FORM

Positive

I**'ve got**	
You**'ve got**	
He**'s**/She**'s**/It**'s got**	a big family.
We**'ve got**	
They**'ve got**	

- *'ve got* and *'s got* are the short forms of *have got* and *has got.* You usually use the short forms in informal spoken and written English.

Negative

I **haven't got**	
You **haven't got**	
He/She/It **hasn't got**	a mobile phone.
We **haven't got**	any pets.
They **haven't got**	

- You often use *any* with the negative forms of *have got* and plural nouns.

Questions and short answers

Have	I/you/we/they	**got** a lot of gadgets?
Has	he/she/it	**got** a mobile phone?

Yes,	you/I/we/they	**have.**
	he/she/it	**has.**
No,	you/I/we/they	**haven't.**
	he/she/it	**hasn't.**

WATCH OUT! You never use short forms in positive short answers:
Yes, I have. (not ~~Yes, I've.~~)

Present simple positive

USE

Use the present simple to talk about
- things that are generally true:
  It **snows** a lot in the winter.
- habits and routines:
  We **watch** television in the evening.

FORM

Positive

- The present simple for *I, you, we* and *they* is the same. For the *he/she/it* forms, add *-s, -es* or *-ies* to the verb.

I/You/We/They	**eat**	lunch at school.
He/She/It	**chats**	online.

Spelling: *he/she/it* forms

- If a verb ends in *-ch, -s, -sh, -x* or *-o*, add *-es*:
  My aunt **teaches** English at a school in town.
  Ingrid **goes** to a computer club after school.
- If a verb ends in a consonant and *-y*, change the *-y* into *-i* and add *-es*:
  My brother **studies** hard.

Prepositions of time

USE AND FORM

- Use *on* for days and dates:
  I call my grandparents **on Sundays**.
  My birthday is **on February 27**.
- Use *in* for months, years, seasons, *the morning/afternoon/evening*:
  Summer starts **in June** here.
  It gets very cold **in winter**.
- Use *at* for *(mid)night, lunchtime, the weekend, o'clock* (and other times):
  We go to the cinema **at the weekend**.
  School finishes **at 3.30**.

Present simple with adverbs of frequency

USE

- Use the present simple with adverbs of frequency to say how often you do things:
  My sister **never tidies** her room.
  We **sometimes watch** films in the evenings.
  My dad **usually cooks** dinner.
- The main adverbs of frequency are (in order of frequency):

0%	never
	hardly ever
	sometimes
	often
	usually, normally
100%	always

- Adverbs of frequency usually go **before** the main verb:
  I **sometimes help** my dad with the cooking.
- Adverbs of frequency go **after** *am/are/is/can*:
  Her room's **always** in a mess.

Present simple negative, questions and short answers

USE

Use the present simple to talk about
- things that are generally true:
  *I **don't like** tomatoes.*
  *Syed **doesn't think** his school is different.*
- habits and routines:
  *I **don't walk** to school. I go by bus.*
  *What **do** you **have** for lunch at school?*

FORM

Negative

- Form the present simple negative with *don't (do not)* or *doesn't (does not)* + verb.

I/You/We/They	don't	eat lunch	at school.
He/She/It	doesn't	play football	after school.

WATCH OUT! In negative sentences, don't add *-s* to the verb after *doesn't*:
*He doesn't **speak** French. (not ~~He doesn't speaks French.~~)*

Questions and short answers

- Form questions in the present simple with *do/ does* + subject + verb.

Do	I/you/we/they	study geography?
Does	he/she/it	speak English?

Yes,	you/I/we/they	do.
	he/she/it	does.
No,	you/I/we/they	don't.
	he/she/it	doesn't.

Question words

- To ask questions in the present simple, use question word (*where, who, what, when, how, which, why*) + *do/does* + subject + verb:
  *When **do you go** to bed?*
  *How **do you travel** to school?*

Possessive *'s* and *whose*

USE

- Use possessive *'s* and *whose* to talk about possessions or relationships:
  ***Whose** jacket is this?*
  It's Natasha's. (The jacket belongs to Natasha.)

FORM

- Use singular noun + *'s*:
  It's Natasha's jacket. (Natasha + 's + jacket)
- Use regular plural noun + *s'*:
  That's the teachers' car park over there. (teachers + s' + car park)
- Use *'s* for irregular plural nouns such as *children, people, women, men*:
  The children's clothes were all over the floor.

WATCH OUT! Notice the difference between possessive *'s* and the short form of *is – 's*:
Are those Harry's trainers?
Harry's 14 years old.

Possessive pronouns

USE

- Use a possessive pronoun in place of a possessive adjective (*my, your*) + noun:
  *It's her jacket. It's **hers**.*
  *That's my phone. It's **mine**.*

FORM

Possessive adjectives	Possessive pronouns
my	mine
your	yours
his/her	his/hers
our	ours
their	theirs

Present continuous

USE

- Use the present continuous to talk about things in progress now or around now:
  I'm doing my homework.
  It isn't raining now. Let's go out.
  What are you listening to?
  Are you watching television?
- You often use time expressions such as *now, right now* and *at the moment* with the present continuous:
  *I'm reading a book **right now**.*

FORM

Positive

- Form the present continuous with *be* + *-ing* form of the verb.

I'm You're He's/She's	waiting	for the bus.
It's	raining.	
We're They're	surfing	the internet.

- You usually use the short forms of *be* in the present continuous:
  He's riding his bike.

Spelling

- If a verb ends in -e, remove the final -e before adding -ing:
  take – taking   use – using
- If a verb ends in a vowel (eg *i, a, o*) and a consonant (eg *m, p, t*), double the consonant before adding -ing:
  swim – swimming   shop – shopping
- If a verb ends in -l, double the -l:
  travel – travelling
- If a verb ends in -ie, change the -ie to -ying:
  lie – lying

Negative

- Form the present continuous negative with *be* + *not* + *-ing* form of the verb.

I'm not You aren't He/She isn't	playing	video games.
It isn't	working.	
We aren't They aren't	meeting	friends.

Questions and short answers

- Form present continuous questions with *be* + subject + *-ing* form of the verb.

Am	I	listening to music?	Yes, you are. / No, you're not.
Are	you		Yes, I am. / No, I'm not.
Is	he/she	playing football?	Yes, he/she is. / No, he/she isn't.
	it	raining?	Yes, it is. / No, it isn't.
Are	we/they	sending an email?	Yes, we/they are. / No, we/they aren't.

- You can also use question words (*What, Who, Where, How*, etc) before *be*:
  What are you doing right now?

WATCH OUT! You never use short forms in positive short answers:
  *Yes, **I am**.* (not *Yes, I'm.*)

Present continuous and present simple

- Use the present continuous to talk about things in progress now or around now and the present simple for habits, routines and things that are generally true:
  *We **usually do** gymnastics on Fridays but today **we're playing** basketball.*
- Use time expressions, such as *this week, right now, at the moment, today* or *now* with the present continuous:
  *I'm **listening** to their new album **at the moment**.*
- Use time expressions such as *this week, usually, on Thursdays, sometimes, never* and *always* with the present simple:
  *I have violin lessons **on Wednesdays** after school.*

A lot of, much, many, some and any

Countable nouns

- are nouns you can count:
  potato, vegetable, chip, etc
- use *a(n)* or *the* in the singular:
  *I usually eat **an apple** every day.*
- have a singular and a plural form:
  tomato   tomatoes

Uncountable nouns

- are nouns you can't count:
  meat, cheese, bread, etc
- don't have a plural form:
  *There is a lot of **cheese** in the fridge.*
  – You can't say *one meat, two meats*, etc.
- Some more common uncountable nouns are:
  food, salad, pasta, spaghetti, soup, milk, juice, fruit, rice.

a lot of, much and *many*

- Use *a lot of* to describe a large quantity of something. You can use this with both countable and uncountable nouns:
  *We've got **a lot of tomatoes.***
  *There is **a lot of bread**.*
- Use *How many* or *How much* to ask about quantity. Use *How many* for countable nouns and *How much* for uncountable nouns:
  ***How many eggs** do we need?*
  ***How much soup** is there?*
- Use *not + many* with countable nouns and *not + much* with uncountable nouns to talk about a small amount of something in negative sentences:
  *We haven't got **many eggs**.*
  *There isn't **much cheese**.*

any

- Use *any* in negative sentences to talk about zero amounts.
- You can use *any* with both countable and uncountable nouns:
  *There aren't **any onions**.*
  *We haven't got **any bread**.*
- Use *any* with countable and uncountable nouns to ask about quantity:
  *Have we got **any milk**?*
  *Are there **any eggs** in the fridge?*

some

- Use *some* to describe an amount that is not big and not small.
- You can use *some* with countable and uncountable nouns:
  *We've got **some bananas**.*
  *There's **some salad** in the fridge.*
- You can also use *some* when making offers or requests. You can use it with countable and uncountable nouns:
  *Would you like **some chips**?*
  *Can I have **some pasta**?*

Like + -ing

USE

- Use *like, love, enjoy + -ing* to talk about your likes:
  *I **like listening** to music.*
  *I **love chatting** to my friends online.*
- *Like* and *enjoy* have a similar meaning. *Love* means to 'like something a lot'.
- Use *hate, dislike, don't like + -ing* to talk about your dislikes:
  *I **hate tidying** my room.*
  *I **don't like going** to bed early.*
- *Don't like* and *dislike* have a similar meaning. *Hate* means to 'not like something a lot'.

FORM

- Use *like, don't like, enjoy, dislike, hate, love*, etc with a noun:
  *I **love** pasta.*
  *I **hate** fish.*
- Use *like, don't like, enjoy, dislike, hate, love*, etc with a verb + *-ing*:
  *I **enjoy reading** magazines.*
  *I **don't like going** shopping.*

Can/can't for ability

USE

- Use *can/can't* to talk about the things we have the ability or time to do:
  *I **can** play tennis.*
  *I **can't** sing very well.*

FORM

- The form stays the same. *Can* and *can't* are the same for *I, you, he/she/it, we* and *they.*

I		
You	can/ can't	meet you tomorrow.
He/She/It		
We		
They		

Questions and short answers

- Form questions by changing the word order:
  ***Can you** play the guitar?*

Can	I/you/we/ they	sing well?	Yes, I/you/we/they **can**.
			No, I/you/we/they **can't**.
	he/she/it		Yes, he/she/it **can**.
			No, he/she/it **can't**.

Adverbs of manner

USE

- Use adverbs to say how you do something:
  *I can't play tennis very **well**.*
  *Gregory talks very **loudly**.*
  *Can you get up **early**?*

FORM

- Form adverbs by adding *-ly* to the adjective:
  loud > loudly
- Some adverbs don't change:
  hard > hard   fast > fast   early > early
  late > late
- Some adverbs are irregular:
  good > well

Spelling

- Most adjectives add *-ly*:
  *quick > quick**ly***
- If an adjective ends in *-y*, drop the *-y* and add *-ily*:
  *easy > eas**ily***

Have to and *don't have to*

USE

- Use *have/has to* + verb to say something is necessary:
  *Players **have to** hit the ball with the bat.*
- Use *don't/doesn't* + *have to* + verb to say something isn't necessary:
  *They **don't have to** run fast.*

FORM
Positive

I/You/We/They	**have to**	train hard.
He/She/It	**has to**	

Negative

I/You/We/They	**don't have to**	buy any special equipment.
He/She	**doesn't have to**	

Questions and short answers

- Form questions with *do/does* + subject + *have to* + verb.

Do I/ you/ we/they	have to	train hard?	Yes, I/we/they **do**. No, I/we/they **don't**.
Does he/she			Yes, he/she **does**. No, he/she **doesn't**.

Was/were; ago

USE

- Use the past simple of *be* to talk about situations in the past:
  I **was** born in London.
  My sister **wasn't** at the party last week.
  My parents **were** at work yesterday.

FORM

Positive

- The positive form of the past simple of *be* is *was* or *were*.

I/He/She/It	**was**	late for
You/We/They	**were**	school.

Negative

- The negative form of the past simple of *be* is *wasn't* or *weren't*.

I/He/She/It	**wasn't** (was not)	at school yesterday.
You/We/They	**weren't** (were not)	

Questions and short answers

- To form questions, use *was/were* + subject.

Were you		Yes, I **was**. No, I **wasn't**.
Was he/she/it	at computer club yesterday?	Yes, he/she/it **was**. No, he/she/it **wasn't**.
Were we/they		Yes, we/they **were**. No, we/they **weren't**.

ago

- Use a time period + *ago* to talk about *when* something happened in relation to today:
  I was at primary school **three years ago**.
  My parents were at work **an hour ago**.

Past simple positive

USE

- Use the past simple to talk about completed actions in the past:
  Yesterday I **went** to school, **saw** my friends and **did** my lessons.
  Last night I **ate** dinner and **watched** TV.
- You often use these time expressions with the past simple:

yesterday	last night/week/month/year
on Monday	in October an hour/two
weeks/three years ago	
in 2013	an hour/two months later

FORM

Regular verbs

- Form the past simple of regular verbs with verb + *ed*. It is the same for all persons.

Affirmative I/You/He/She/It/We/They	**started**	secondary school in 2013.

Spelling

- If a verb ends in *-y*, change the *y* into *i* before adding *-ed*:
  study – stud**ied**
  But not if there is a vowel before the *-y*:
  play – play**ed** (not ~~plaid~~)
- If a verb ends in a vowel (eg *o*) and a consonant (eg *p*, *t*), double the consonant:
  stop – stop**ped**
- If a verb ends in *-l*, double the *l*:
  travel – travel**led**

Irregular verbs

- Many verbs are irregular in the past simple. You have to learn these:
  can – **could**   eat – **ate**   go – **went**

See page 140 for a list of irregular verbs in the past simple.

Past simple negative

USE

- Use the past simple to talk about completed actions in the past:
  *I **didn't see** him yesterday.*
  *We **didn't have** a great time on holiday.*

FORM

Negative

- Form the past simple negative with *didn't* (*did not*) + verb.

I/You/He/She/We/They	didn't (did not)	feel	well.

- Use the short form *didn't* in informal speech and informal writing.

Past simple questions and short answers

USE

- Use the past simple to ask about completed actions in the past:
  *Where **did** you **go** on holiday?*
  ***Did** you **go** by plane?*

FORM

- Form past simple questions with: *Did* + subject + verb.

Did	you/he/she/it/we/they	have a good time?
Yes,	I/you/he/she/it/we/they	did.
No,	I/you/he/she/it/we/they	didn't.

- You can also use question words (*What, Who, Where, How,* etc) before *did*:
  ***Where did you go** last night?*

WATCH OUT! Don't use the past simple positive form in negatives and questions:
*I didn't **watch** TV last night.* (not ~~I didn't **watched** TV last night.~~)
*Did you **take** a lot of photos?* (not ~~Did you **took** a lot of photos?~~)

Comparative adjectives

USE

- Use comparative adjectives to compare two things:
  *The shopping centre is **cheaper than** the local shop.*
  *These trainers are **more expensive than** those ones.*

FORM

- To form the comparative of most adjectives, add -er.
- See the table for other spelling changes.
- Use *than* after the comparative adjective:
  *The online store has a bigger selection **than** the shop in town.*

Word type	Adjective	Comparative adjective
One syllable	fast	fast**er**
One syllable ending in -e	late	lat**er**
One syllable ending in one vowel + one consonant	big	bi**gger**
Two syllables ending in -y	busy	busi**er**
Two or more syllables	expensive	**more expensive**
Two or more syllables ending in -er, -et, -ow or -le	clever	clever**er**

WATCH OUT! Some comparative adjectives are irregular:

Adjective	Comparative adjective
good	**better**
bad	**worse**
far	**further**

Superlative adjectives

USE

- Use superlative adjectives to compare one thing with all the other things in a group:
  *The sports shop in the town centre has **the biggest** selection of trainers.*
  *The café next to school makes **the best** milkshakes.*

FORM

- To form the superlative of most adjectives, use the + adjective + -est.
- See the table for other spelling changes.

Word type	Adjective	Superlative adjective
One syllable	fast	**the fastest**
One syllable ending in -e	late	**the latest**
One syllable ending in one vowel + one consonant	big	**the biggest**
Two syllables ending in -y	busy	**the busiest**
Two or more syllables	comfortable	**the most comfortable**
Two or more syllables ending in -er, -et, -ow or -le	clever	**the cleverest**

WATCH OUT! Some superlative adjectives are irregular:

Adjective	Superlative adjective
good	**the best**
bad	**the worst**
far	**the furthest**

Going to

USE

- Use *be going to* + verb to talk about plans for the future:
  I'm going to visit my grandad this weekend.
  We're going to watch the fireworks this evening.
  What are you going to do after school?

FORM

Positive

I'm		
You're/We're/They're	going to	meet my friends tomorrow.
He's/She's/It's		

Negative

I'm not		
You/We/ They aren't	going to	play on the computer.
He/She/It isn't		

Questions and short answers

- Form questions with *be* + subject + *going to* + verb.

Am I			Yes, I am. No, I'm not.
Is he/she/it	going to	watch the concert?	Yes, he/she/it is. No, he/she/it isn't.
Are you/ we/ they			Yes, you/we/they are. No, you/we/they aren't.

Will for predictions

USE

- Use *will/will not* + verb for predictions about the future:
  There will be a lot of people at Anna's party tomorrow night.
  Will the weather be OK at the weekend?
- You can also use *I think* or *I don't think* with *will* if you're not sure:
  I think I'll get good marks in my English test.
  I don't think my sister will lend me her new jacket.

FORM

Positive

- *'ll* (*will*) + verb does not change with *he/she/it*.

I'll	
You'll	
He'll/She'll/It'll	stay at home this weekend.
We'll	
They'll	

Negative

- *won't* (*will not*) + verb does not change with *he/she/it*.

I won't	
You won't	
He/She/It won't	go out.
We won't	
They won't	

Questions and short answers

Will I		
Will you		
Will he/she/it	play a lot of video games?	Yes, I/you/he/she/it/we/they will. No, I/you/he/she/it/we/they won't.
Will we		
Will they		

Page 10

RECALL

IN TOWN

flat	city	school
house	café	sports centre
building	cinema	swimming pool
town/city centre	park	zoo
town	restaurant	

WORK WITH WORDS ▶▶▶

TIP: Draw pictures or icons to help you remember words (eg café: ☕).

TASK: Draw small pictures for the 'In town' words.

Pages 10 and 11

PLACES IN A TOWN

airport
castle
library
museum
shopping centre
square
stadium
station
theme park
tower

GO BEYOND

Write what you can do at each place, eg _Airport: You can travel to other countries from here._

Page 14

RECALL

GO BEYOND

1 **Circle the adjective in the second list.**
2 **Tick (✓) your family members in both lists.**

FAMILY (1)

brother	grandfather
child	grandma
dad	grandmother
father	mother
grandad	mum
grandchild	sister

FAMILY (2)

aunt	husband
cousin	married
daughter	parents
granddaughter	son
grandparents	uncle
grandson	wife

NEW WORDS IN UNIT 1

canal	guidebook	turn
corner	health	twin town / sister city
directions	miss	wheel
greet	puppet	
guide	straight on	

Page 20

RECALL

DAILY ROUTINE
finish school
get up
go to bed
go to school
have breakfast/lunch/dinner

WORK WITH WORDS

TIP: To help you remember activities, note when you do them.

TASK: Think of two days when you do the 'Daily routine' activities at different times.

Pages 20 and 21

DAILY ACTIVITIES
brush my hair
clean my teeth
do my homework
get dressed
get home
get to school
go home
have a shower
pack my bag
wake up

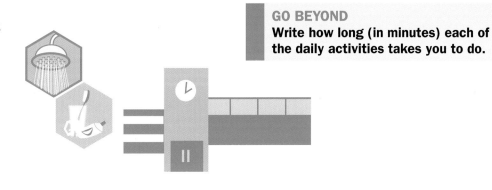

GO BEYOND
Write how long (in minutes) each of the daily activities takes you to do.

Page 24

RECALL

ROOMS
bathroom
bedroom
dining room
hall
kitchen
living room

FURNITURE AND OTHER THINGS IN THE HOME
armchair
bookcase
carpet
cooker
cupboard
curtains
fridge
lamp
shelf (shelves)
sofa
wardrobe
washing machine

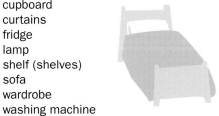

GO BEYOND
1 **Draw a floor plan of your house or flat, showing the rooms.**
2 **Draw the pieces of furniture and other things in the home on the floor plan, and then label them with their names.**

NEW WORDS IN UNIT 2

24-hour clock	celebrate	label	rain (v)	timetable
Arctic Circle	come up	lunchtime	season	warm
barbecue	equator	midnight	shine	windy
beach	go down	Northern Lights	snow (v)	winter
bored	hungry	organised	space	
box	(in) a mess	quiet	the school year	

WORDS & BEYOND

Page 32

RECALL

THINGS YOU DO AT SCHOOL	THINGS YOU USE IN CLASS	THINGS YOUR TEACHER USES IN CLASS	THINGS YOU SEE ON THE CLASSROOM WALL
answer questions	an exercise book	a board/blackboard	a clock
do exercises	a pen/pencil	a book	a poster
do sports	a rubber/eraser	a computer	a shelf
do tests	a student's book / coursebook	a desk	a timetable
go on the internet	a workbook	a pen	
play games			
watch videos			
write essays			

WORK WITH WORDS »

TIP: Think of words you associate with different places and make lists in a vocabulary notebook. Add new words to the lists.

TASK: Think of a special place. Make a list of words you associate with the place.

Pages 32 and 33

SCHOOL SUBJECTS

art
design & technology
drama
English
geography
history
IT (information technology)
languages
maths
music
PE (physical education)
science

GO BEYOND

Tick (✓) the school subjects you like and put a cross (✗) next to the ones you don't like.

Page 36

RECALL

GO BEYOND

What do you wear at these times of year – winter, spring, summer, autumn? Use adverbs of frequency: *sometimes*, *often*, etc.

CLOTHES	CLOTHES AND ACCESSORIES
bag	backpack
dress	belt
hat	coat
jacket	earrings
jeans	gloves
shirt	hoody
shoes	jumper
skirt	scarf
socks	shorts
sunglasses	tie
trainers	tracksuit top/bottoms
trousers	
T-shirt	

NEW WORDS IN UNIT 3

amazing	orange juice	stuff
break	rock music	stripes
classical music	rules	typical
joke	running track	uniform

Page 42

RECALL

FREE-TIME ACTIVITIES

go on the internet
go shopping
go swimming
go to the cinema
listen to music
meet friends

play football
play the piano
play video games
read a book
ride a bike
watch television

WORK WITH WORDS >>>

TIP: Think of different words you can use with the same verbs (*play football, play the piano*, etc).

TASK: Write another word for each of the verbs in the list.

Pages 42 and 43

ACTIVITY VERBS

arrive, leave
come, go
go out, stay in
laugh, cry
open, close
put on, take off
send, get
stand, sit
start, end
talk to, listen to

GO BEYOND
Write five sentences using the verbs with an adverb of frequency: *sometimes, usually, often, always, never*.

Page 46

PLACES IN PUBLIC BUILDINGS

coffee shop
entrance
first floor
gift shop
ground floor
information desk
lift
stairs
ticket office
toilets

GO BEYOND
Choose four places from the list and write three things you usually find there.

NEW WORDS IN UNIT 4

announcement
cake
exhibition
event

festival
hip hop
look forward to
park (a car)

performer
playground
social networking
tour

truth
umbrella

WORDS &BEYOND

Page 54

RECALL

FOOD AND DRINK

apple	chicken	fruit	milk	rice
banana	coffee	grapes	mineral water	salad
burger	drink	ice cream	orange	sandwich
bread	egg	juice	pizza	steak
cheese	fish	meat	pasta	tea

WORK WITH WORDS ▶▶▶

TIP: Write the English words for things on sticky notes. Put them on food, clothes, things in the house, …

TASK: At home, put notes on things in your fridge or kitchen cupboard. Or put the notes on the fridge door or cupboard door with small drawings.

Pages 54 and 55

FOOD AND DRINK

butter		onion	
cake		potato	
carrot		soup	
chips		sweets	
chocolate		tomato	
cola		yoghurt	

GO BEYOND

Tick (✓) the things that you like. Cross (✗) the things that you don't like.

Page 58

LIFESTYLE ADJECTIVES

active
busy
fit
ill
lazy
lucky
stressed
tired
unhappy
well

GO BEYOND

Find two pairs of opposites in the list of adjectives.

NEW WORDS IN UNIT 5

a kind of	dish	lemon	packed lunch	survey
brain	energy	lifestyle	respect	taco
block	face to face	menu	sauce	unhealthy
dessert	healthy	news	search	

Page 64

RECALL

SPORTS

baseball	sailing
basketball	skiing
cycling	surfing
football	swimming
golf	tennis
hockey	table tennis
horse-riding	volleyball
ice skating	

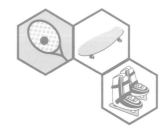

WORK WITH WORDS

TIP: Make a list of words with the same sounds.

TASK: Find three other words in **RECALL** with the /eɪ/ sound in *baseball*. <u>Underline</u> the part of the word with the sound.

Pages 64 and 65

SPORTS AND GAMES

American football	gymnastics
badminton	ice hockey
bowling	rugby
cards	skateboarding
chess	snowboarding
cricket	video games

GO BEYOND
In which country or countries are the sports and games very popular?

Page 68

GAMES VERBS

climb
destroy
hit
jump (over)
look for
lose
move
shoot
throw
win

GO BEYOND
Write a noun after each verb, eg *climb a mountain*.

NEW WORDS IN UNIT 6

ability	comedian	superstar
admire	competitive	train
agent	competitor	trainer
coach	cook	viewer

Page 76

RECALL

DATES

10.06 / 10th June: Say _the tenth of June._
1999: Say _nineteen ninety nine._
2001: Say _two thousand and one._
2014: Say _twenty fourteen._

WORK WITH WORDS

TIP: Practise saying the date in English when you wake up in the morning.

TASK: Write a list of important dates for you. Practise saying them.

Pages 76 and 77

TIMES OF LIFE

baby
child
teenager
middle-aged
pensioner
young adult

be born
grow up
get old
die

GO BEYOND

1 For each time of life, write the name of somebody you know.
2 Write four sentences with each of the four verbs.

Page 80

PERSONALITY ADJECTIVES

calm
cheerful
cool
friendly
funny
nice
polite
rude
serious
shy

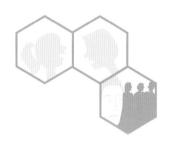

GO BEYOND

Describe two friends or family members with some of the words.

NEW WORDS IN UNIT 7

age	creative	informal	recipe	simple
ago	diary	life	rest	timeline
calendar	education	medicine	sail	thousand
celebration	field	millennium	ship	
century	guess	million		

Page 86

RECALL

WEATHER

cloud, cloudy
cold
fog, foggy
hot
rain, rainy (it's raining)
sun, sunny
warm
wind, windy

WORK WITH WORDS ▶▶▶

TIP: You can add *-y* to some nouns to make adjectives (*cloud*, *cloudy*). Learn them together.

TASK: Make adjectives from these nouns: *fun*, *hair*, *health*, *luck*, *noise*, *snow*. Use a dictionary to check the spelling.

Pages 86 and 87

PREPOSITIONS OF MOVEMENT

across
along
around
down
into
out of
past
through
towards
up

GO BEYOND
Describe your journey from home to school using prepositions of movement.

Page 90

FORMS OF TRANSPORT

boat
coach
helicopter
lorry
motorbike
plane
ship
train
tram
underground

GO BEYOND
Choose two or three forms of transport. Write one good and one bad thing about each one.

NEW WORDS IN UNIT 8

bazaar	island	sightseeing	toothbrush
check in	journey	sign	toothpaste
check out	(make a) reservation	single	twin
double	mosque	tent	
flight	pyjamas		

WORDS &BEYOND

Page 98

THINGS YOU CAN BUY AT A SHOPPING CENTRE

Clothes and accessories: See Unit 3
Electronic devices: *mobile phone, computer, laptop, tablet, games console, camera*
Food: See Unit 5
Furniture: See Unit 2
Instruments: *guitar, drum(s), keyboard, piano, violin*
Pets: *cat, dog, fish, rabbit, mouse, hamster*

WORK WITH WORDS

TIP: Make revision cards. Write a category on one side and words in that category on the other.

TASK: Make revision cards for some of the RECALL words. Then pick up a card. How many words can you remember in that category?

Pages 98 and 99

SHOPS
baker's
bookshop
butcher's
chemist
clothes shop
department store
electronics shop
music shop
newsagent
pet shop
sports shop
toy shop

GO BEYOND
What different shops do you go to? Write their names and what you buy in each one.

Page 102

MONEY AND MEASUREMENTS
cent
dollar
euro
kilogram / kilo
kilometre
litre
metre
mile
pence / p
pound

GO BEYOND
Match the money and measurements to these symbols and abbreviations:
$ £   p   kg   lb   km   m   l

NEW WORDS IN UNIT 9

actively	cost (v)	inch	quality
brand	far	original	roll
brown bread	follow fashion	pay (v)	save
chocolate bar	foot	pint	spend
compare	gallon	price tag	

Page 108:

SPECIAL DAYS
give/get presents
have a party, a special meal
play the drums, the guitar, music

WORK WITH WORDS 》》

TIP: Learn verb + noun combinations.   **TASK:** Think of two other words you can use after the verbs in RECALL.

Pages 108 and 109
FESTIVALS

Nouns	Verbs
candles	celebrate
celebration	decorate
costume	invite
decorations	wish
fireworks	
parade	

GO BEYOND
Write 50 words about a celebration or party you had or are going to have. Use as many 'festival' words as you can.

Page 112
FEELINGS

afraid	interested
angry	nervous
bored	relaxed
embarrassed	surprised
excited	worried

GO BEYOND
Write about the last time you had three of these feelings. Explain why.

NEW WORDS IN UNIT 10

bonfire	festival	pirate	RSVP
calendar	flag	plan	solution
Congratulations!	giant	positive	spider
dress code	Good luck!	predict	tomorrow
feeling	mistake		

IRREGULAR VERBS

base form	past simple	past participle
be	was/were	been
be born	was/were born	has/have been born
become	became	become
break	broke	broken
bring	brought	brought
buy	bought	bought
can	could	been able to
catch	caught	caught
choose	chose	chosen
come	came	come
cost	cost	cost
do	did	done
drive	drove	driven
eat	ate	eaten
feel	felt	felt
find	found	found
fly	flew	flown
forget	forgot	forgotten
get	got	got
give	gave	given
go	went	gone
grow	grew	grown
have	had	had
hear	heard	heard
hit	hit	hit
know	knew	known
learn	learnt/learned	learnt/learned
let	let	let

base form	past simple	past participle
leave	left	left
lose	lost	lost
make	made	made
meet	met	met
pay	paid	paid
put	put	put
read	read	read
ride	rode	ridden
run	ran	run
say	said	said
see	saw	seen
sell	sold	sold
send	sent	sent
shoot	shot	shot
sing	sang	sung
sit	sat	sat
speak	spoke	spoken
stand	stood	stood
take	took	taken
tell	told	told
think	thought	thought
throw	threw	thrown
understand	understood	understood
wake	woke	woken
wear	wore	worn
write	wrote	written
win	won	won

STUDENT A (AND C)

UNIT 1 GRAMMAR 1

Page 13, Exercise 6

Student A

UNIT 8 GRAMMAR 2

Page 91, Exercise 5

Student A

Write the quiz questions about Tintin and the Belgian artist Hergé in the past simple.

1 Who / Hergé / create?
2 When / the character / first appear?
3 What / be / his dog's name?

UNIT 2 SPEAKING

Page 27, Exercise 7

Students A and C

1 a Complete the information by asking Students B and D questions.

> **UK Travel app**
> Time now: _____
> Next train to Manchester: _____

b Student A: Ask Student C how much time you've got. Decide what to do in that time.

2 Answer Students B and D's questions. Use this information:

> **UK Travel app**
> Time now: 09:30
> Next bus to London: 10:08

Write the quiz answers in the past simple.

a He _____ (go) to Peru.
b He _____ (not answer) that question.
c He _____ (write) 29 stories between 1930 and 1976.

All students

UNIT 1 SPEAKING

Page 17, Exercise 5

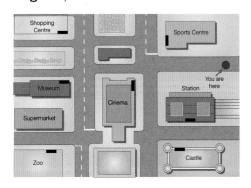

UNIT 7 SPEAKING

Page 83, Exercise 6a

He walked …

He held the door for …

People went …

The last person …

The door …

UNIT 1 GRAMMAR 1

Page 13, Exercise 6

Student B

UNIT 8 GRAMMAR 2

Page 91, Exercise 5

Student B

Write the quiz questions about Tintin and the Belgian artist Hergé in the past simple.

1 How many / Tintin books / Hergé / write?
2 Where / Tintin / go / in *Prisoners of the Sun*?
3 Why / Hergé / give / him the name Tintin?

UNIT 2 SPEAKING

Page 27, Exercise 7

Students B and D

1 a Complete the information by asking Students A and C questions.

> **UK Travel app**
> Time now: ....
> Next bus to London: ....

b Student B: Ask Student C how much time you've got. Decide what to do in that time.

2 Answer Students A and C's questions. Use this information:

> **UK Travel app**
> Time now: 19:45
> Next train to Manchester: 20:15

Write the quiz answers in the past simple.

a He first _____ (appear) on 10 January 1929.
b His name _____ (be) Milou in the original version and Snowy in the English version.
c He _____ (create) the character of Tintin.

Answers

UNIT 5 VOCABULARY

Page 55, Exercise 7b

> **HEALTHY AND HAPPY SURVEY**
>
> • Count your partner's points: A=3, B=2, C=1
> • Check your partner's score.
> 7–9 Great – you're healthy and happy! A new report shows that a healthy teenager is a happy teenager.
> 4–6 You're quite healthy – do you feel happy? Try and eat more fruit and vegetables and do more healthy activities.
> 1–3 Do more sport and eat more healthy food – you'll feel happier!

UNIT 7 VOCABULARY

Page 76, Exercise 1b

1 *The twenty-first of August, eighteen forty-five.*

2 *The fifteenth of April, nineteen twelve.*

3 *The thirty-first of December, nineteen ninety-nine.*

4 *The first of January, two thousand.*

5 *The twelfth of December, twenty thirteen.*

UNIT 6 VOCABULARY

Page 64, Exercise 2

1 gymnastics

2 badminton

3 bowling

4 ice hockey

5 chess

6 rugby

STEP-BY-STEP PROJECTS

Download more information from www.macmillanbeyond.com

MAKE A MAP

- Choose a name for a new town – *Futuretown, Our world ...*
- Make a list of places and services.
- Design a map. Use different icons and colours.

Units 1 & 2

KEEP A DIARY

- Make a list of tasks – *write a poem in English, be nice to people ...*
- Make a diary and write a task on each day.
- Write about each day and try to do the task.

Units 7 & 8

RECORD N AUDIO TOUR

- Choose a place for your tour – *the school, a museum, a park ...*
- Write the script and describe the things you see.
- Read or record your audio tour.

Units 3 & 4

DESIGN A SHOPPING CENTRE

- Choose the shops – *sports shop, clothes shop ...*
- Make a plan of the centre with the different shops.
- Prepare a TV or radio ad for the shopping centre.

Units 9 & 10

O A FOOD SURVEY

- Choose a topic for your survey – *school food, favourite food, snacks ...*
- Write the questions and choices for the answers.
- Interview other students and look at the results.

Units 5 & 6

Macmillan Education
4 Crinan Street
London N1 9XW
A division of Macmillan Publishers Limited

Companies and representatives throughout the world

ISBN 978-0-230-41017-6

Text © Robert Campbell, Rob Metcalf and Rebecca Robb Benne 2015
Design and illustration © Macmillan Publishers Limited 2015

The authors have asserted their rights to be identified as the authors of this work in accordance with the Copyright, Designs and Patents Act 1988.

First published 2015

Designed by emc design ltd

Illustrated by Tom Croft pp13, 114, 141 (tl), 142 (tl); Sophie Escabasse pp16; Venitia Dean (Advocate-Art) pp31, 58, 112; Cyrus Deboo pp10, 20, 46, 59 (thumbs up/down), 90; Stephen Dew pp36, 63, 86 (temperature icons); Mark Duffin p 103 (phones); Sally Elford pp10 (header graphics), 20 (header graphics), 30-31 (graphic icons), 32 (header graphics), 42 (header graphics), 52-53 (graphic icons), 54 (header graphics), 64 (header graphics), 74-75 (graphic icons), 76 (header graphics), 86 (header graphics), 96-97 (graphic icons), 98 (header graphics), 103 (l), 108 (header graphics), 118-119 (graphic icons), 130, 139 (graphic icons); Kev Hopgood pp78, 80, 141 (b); Caron Painter (Sylvie Poggio Artists) pp15, 41, 51, 59, 68; Carl Pearce (Advocate-Art) pp6, 7, 8, 9; Zara Picken pp32-33, 73; Dave Shephard (The Bright Agency) pp37, 45, 95, 96 (main image); 111; Tony Wilkins pp19, 110; Paul Williams (Sylvie Poggio Artists) pp54-55.

Cover design by emc design ltd
Cover photographs by Alamy/Mediacolor's, Alamy/Bhandol
Picture research by Emily Taylor

The authors would like to thank all the team at Macmillan in the UK, Mexico, Poland, Spain and the rest of the world for everything they've done to make Beyond possible. Special thanks to our commissioning editor, managing editor and our publisher for their endless hard work and encouragement. We'd like to thank Studio 8 for their creative work on the drama group videos and EMC for coming up with the Beyond design concept. We'd also like to thank all the teachers and other individuals who have contributed to the course whose names appear on this page. A special thank you to Brian Robb for allowing us to use the photos of him on pages 76-77. Finally, we'd like to thank our friends and families for all their support.

The authors and publishers would like to express thanks to all those who contributed to the development and formation of Beyond. In particular, we would like to thank the following teachers, contacts and reviewers: Cristina Moisen Anton, Argelia Solis Arriaga, Krzysztof Bartold, Paweł Bienert, Agnieszka Bojanowska, Samuel Gomez Borobia, Ma. Eugenia Fernandez Castro, Jolanta Chojnacka, Elsa Georgina Cruz, Dominika Dąbrowska, Barbara Dawidowska, Galina Dragunova, Monika Drygiel-Kobylińska, Mauricio Duran, Natalia Evdokimenko, Maria Teresa Velazquez Evers, Marciana Loma-Osorio Fontecha, Monika Fromiczew-Droździńska, Patricia Garcia, Axel Morales Garcia, Miguel Angel Rodriguez Garcia, Aleksandra Gilewska, Joanna Gora, Ewa Gorka, Agata Helwich, Bethsabe Ruiz Herrera, Robert Jadachowski, Patricia Guzman Luis Juan, Anna Kacpura, Ruth Kanter, Regina Kaźmierczuk, Katarzyna Konisiewicz, Maria Koprowska, Bogusława Krajewska, Aldona Krasoń, Joanna Worobiec Kugaj, Joanna Kuligowska, Tadeusz Kur, Maria Kwiatkowska, Josefina Maitret, Claire Manners, Laura Elena Medina, Carmen Garcia Mendez, Iwona Mikucka, Talhia Miranda, Claudia Rangel Miranda, Armando Nieto, Joanna Nowak, Anna Nowakowska, Ewa Nowicka, Anastasia Parshikova, Paloma Carrasco Penalba, Ma. Del Carmen Fernandez Perez, Joanna Płatos, Maria Teresa Portillo, Juan Jose Gomez Ramirez, Aida Rivera, Gabriela Rubio, Gabriela Bourge Ruiz, Irina Sakharova, Małgorzata Sałaj, Patricia Avila Sanchez, Jessica Galvan Sanchez, Miguel Angel Santiago, Karol Sęk, Barbara Sibilska, Tatiana Sinyavina, Agnieszka Śliwowska, Vlada Songailene, Angela Siles Suarez, Beata Świątkowska, Ewelina Szmyd-Patuła, Agnieszka Szymaniak, Jose Luis Vazquez, Irma Velazquez, Małgorzata Walczak, Dariusz Winiarek, Justyna Zdunek, Zofia Żdżarska, Dominika Zięba, Marzena Zieleniewska, Anna Zielińska-Miszczuk, Robert Zielonka.

The authors and publishers would also like to thank the following schools who allowed class observations – MEXICO: Centro de Formacion Escolar Banting, Centro Escolar Las Aguilas, Colegio America, Colegio Axayacatl, Colegio Donato Bramante, Colegio Edgar Morin, Colegio Frances Nueva Santa Maria, Colegio Gesi Secundaria, Colegio Jose Marti S. C., Colegio San Agustin, Colegio Sir Winston Leonard Spencer Churchill De Mexico, Colegios La Salle Boulevares, Cristian Fernandez de Merino, Erasmo De Rotterdam, Escuela De Ruan, Grupo Colegio Rosario Castellanos, Instituto Atenea, Instituto Crisol, Instituto Cultural Americano Mexicano, Instituto Manuel Acosta, Instituto Oriente Arboledas, Instituto Zaragoza, Liceo Americano Frances, Liceo Ibero Mexicano, Liceo Mexicano Japones, Secundaria Simon Bolivar. SPAIN: IES Anselmo Lorenzo, IES Camilo Jose Cela, IES Complutense, IES Joaquin Turina, IES Laguna de Joatzell, IES Luis Garcia Berlanga, IES Manuel de Falla, IES Maximo Trueba. POLAND: Gimnazjum nr 30, Gimnazjum nr 104 Warszawa Wawer, Gimnazjum nv120, Gimnazjum nr 141, Gimnazjum nr 145, Gimnazjum, ul. SZKOLNA 4, Publiczne Gimnazjum w Wiązownie, ZSP w Jazgarzewie. TURKEY: Ahmet Şimşek Koleji, Anabilim Koleji, Buyuk Camlıca Koleji, Doğa Koleji, Kirimli Fazilet Olcay Anatolian High School, Modafen Koleji, Sakıp Sabancı Anadolu Lisesi.

The authors and publishers would like to thank the following for permission to reproduce their photographs:
Alamy/Rudolf Abraham p109(b), Alamy/Amana p20(a), Alamy/Angela Hampton Picture Library p45(cr), Alamy/Art Directors & Trip p92(pyjamas), Alamy/Maxime Bessieres p86(c), Alamy/Big Cheese Photo LLC p25, Alamy/Richard G. Bingham II pp35(br), 40(cr), Alamy/Jeffrey Blackler p99(5), Alamy/Blend Images pp113, 143(cl), Alamy/Kevin Britland p110, Alamy/Paul Broadbent p89, Alamy/Paul Brown p109(c), Alamy/Clynt Garnham Food & Drink p55(a), Alamy/Dominic Cole p24(3), Alamy/Collectiva p92(toothpaste), Alamy/Caroline Cortizo p26(3), Alamy/David Crausby p91(br), Alamy/Ian Dagnall p98(1), Alamy/Daisy Images p94(background), Alamy/

Desintegrator p92(t-shirt), Alamy/Reinhard Dirscherl p88(a), Alamy/Echt p87(f-background), Alamy/Elizabeth Whiting & Associates p28, Alamy/Eyecandy Images p42(c), Alamy/Eye Ubiquitous p55(h), Alamy/Foodstock p78(3), Alamy/Fotomatador p98(3), Alamy/Rostislav Glinsky p11(rollercoaster), Alamy/Graja p143(bl), Alamy/David Gregs p84, Alamy/Howard Harrison p69(tl), Alamy/Hemis p88(b), Alamy/Brent Hofacker p62(tr), Alamy/Chris Howes/Wild Places Photography p30, Alamy/D. Hurst p92(socks), Alamy/Ikon p41, 143(br), Alamy/Imagebroker p45(cl), Alamy/Image Source pp36(c), 36(a) 143(tr), Alamy/Interfoto p91(tml), Alamy/Jaubert Images p75, Alamy/Johner Images p87(f-boy), Alamy/John Kellerman p46(cm), Alamy/Kurtay p109(e), Alamy/Lebrecht Music and Arts Photo Library p90(c), Alamy/Keith Levit p88(cr), Alamy/Luminis p92(trousers), Alamy/Mediablitzimages p92(toothbrush), Alamy/Moodboard p86-87, Alamy/Keith Morris p76(br), Alamy/Ian Nolan p24(1), Alamy/Sergey Novikov p103(tl), Alamy/One-Image Photography p23(tl), Alamy/David Parker p88(c), Alamy/Andrew Paterson p92(t-shirt), Alamy/Trevor Pearson p55(c), Alamy/Photocuisine p55(e), Alamy/Photo Japan p12(bm), Alamy/Phovoir pp24(tr), 65(5), 142(5), Alamy/Gennadiy Poznyakov p37, Alamy/Anton Prado p92(books), Alamy/Redsnapper p26(2), Alamy/Alex Segre p99(4), Alamy/Shapencolour p24(11), Alamy/Vivek Sharma p66(bl), Alamy/Mark Spowart pp64(4), 142(4), Alamy/Christopher Stewart p40(cl), Alamy/Tetra Images p58, Alamy/Texas Stock Photo p35(tr), Alamy/TMI p87(e), Alamy/Travelpix Ltd p79(tr), Alamy/United Archives p90(b), Alamy/VIEW Pictures Ltd pp32-33, 34, 98(2), Alamy/H. Mark Weidman p42(a), 47(tr), Alamy/Alan Williams p55(d, g), Alamy/Zoonar GmbH p143(tl); **BananaStock** p78(6); **Comstock Images** p78(5); **Corbis** p101, Corbis/AID/Amanaimages p14(tcl), Corbis/Altrendo/Juice Images p44, Corbis/Beyond p60(tr), Corbis/Blend Images p106, Corbis/Blue Jean Images pp64(2), 142(2), Corbis/Burger/Phanie p10, Corbis/Kevin Dodge p99(girls), Corbis/Randy Faris pp64(3), 142(3), Corbis/Peter M Fisher p74, Corbis/Yves Forestier/Sygma p72(tr), Corbis/Franz-Marc Frei p10(federation square), Corbis/John Gollings/Arcaid p11(stadium), Corbis/Tim Graham pp22(cm, cl), Corbis/I Love Images p69(cr), Corbis/In Pictures p108-109, Corbis/Dimitri Iundt/TempSport p65(1), 142(1), Corbis/Sean Justice p40(tm), Corbis/KidStock/Blend Images p14(bl), Corbis/Kate Kunz p24(2), Corbis/Tony Kurdzuk/Star Ledger p111, Corbis/Simon Marcus p35(tr), Corbis/Caroline Mowry/Somos Images p20(d), Corbis/Jaak Nilson/Spaces Images p99(6), Corbis/Ocean Images p20(b), 26(bl), 65(6), 142(6), Corbis/Tim Pannell p102, Corbis/Radius Images pp23(cl), 82(tl), Corbis/Brett Stevens/Cultura p103, Corbis/Tetrap15(tr), Corbis/The Food Passionates p56(tr), Corbis/Bob Thomas p69(tr), Corbis/Kim Walker/Robert Harding World Imagery p22(bm); **Fotolibra**/Mark Ferguson pp24(4,8,10); **Getty Images** pp19, 43(b), 70, 78(4), 79(tl), 94(cl), Getty Images/Ac_bnphotos p62(tl), Getty Images/Age Fotostock p18, Getty Images/Amanaimages p67, Getty Images/AWL Images pp94(br), 118, Getty Images/Allan Baxter p11(luna park entrance), Getty Images/Boston Globe p56(tl), Getty Images/Peter Cade p60(tl), Getty Images/Cavan Images p66(bl), Getty Images/Compassionate Eye Foundation p38, Getty Images/Cultura Creative p81, Getty Images/Cultura RF pp14(tr), 26(br), 66(tr), Getty Images/P. Eoche p56(bl), Getty Images/Flickr RF pp23(tr), 56(cr), 108(a), Getty Images/Gerenme p26(1), Getty Images/Glowimages p104, Getty Images/Matt Henry Gunther p20(c), Getty Images/Philip Lee Harvey p42(e), Getty Images/Image Source pp36(b), 43(f), Getty Images/iStockphoto p112, Getty Images/Lonely Planet Images pp10-11(map), 11(museum), 86(b), Getty Images/OJO Images p82(tr), Getty Images/Michael Pasdzior p87(d), Getty Images/Photolibrary p55(f), Getty Images/Mike Powell p43(d), Getty Images/Radius Images p100, Getty Images/Keith Reicher p46(cr), Getty Images/Robin Smith p11(tower), Getty Images/Mike Sonnenberg p54, Getty Images/SSPL/Planet News Archive p90(a), Getty Images/Terry Roberts Photography p97, Getty Images/UIG p12(tr), Getty Images/Uppercut p109(b-inset), Getty Images/Urbancow p46(cl), Getty Images/VM p50, Getty Images/Ken Welch p88(bm), Getty Images/Brad Wilson p26(bm), Getty Images/WireImage p72(bl); **Macmillan Publishers Ltd** p78(2); **Photoshot**/JTB p12(cr); **Plain Picture**/Ableimages p40(tr), Plain Picture/Cultura p82(tm), Plain Picture/Etsa p59, Plain Picture/Johnerp10(br), Plain Picture/Maskot p24(12), Plain Picture/Narratives p24(5,6,7,9), Plain Picture/Sehnaz p14(bcr), Plain Picture/Kniel Synnatzschke p47(cr); **Rex Features**/Keystone p109(d); **Rebecca Robb-Benne** pp76(tr), 77(all images) **Science Photo Library**/NASA p20-21(map); **Stockbyte** p78(1); **SuperStock**/Katiimagebroker p60(tm); **Thinkstock** p92(tablet, phone), Thinkstock/iStock p109(fireworks), Thinkstock/Johnnyscriv p35(tr), Thinkstock/Medioimages/Photodisc p91(tl).

Commissioned photographs by Studio 8 ltd, www.studio-8.com, 01865 842525, pp17 27, 39, 49, 61, 71, 83, 93, 105, 115.

The authors and publishers are grateful for permission to reprint the following copyright material:
Extract from http://www.watershedschool.org © Watershed School, 2014. Reprinted with permission.
Extract from http://www.redbandana.com © Red Bandana Band and Bare Bones Productions, 2013.
Extract from http://www.juditpolgar.com © Judit Polgár, 2012. Reprinted with permission.
Extract from http://www.londoneye.com © EDF Energy London Eye, 2014. Reprinted with permission.
Extract from 'Palle Huld: Actor whose round the world journey was the inspiration for Tintin' by Pierre Perrone. Originally published in The Independent on 14.12.2010. © The Independent 2010. Reprinted with permission.
www.independent.co.uk
Extract from Encyclopedia of Children and Childhood, 1E. © 2004 Gale, a part of Cengage Learning, Inc. Reproduced by permission. www.cengage.com/permissions
Extract from http://www.golowan.org © Golowan Festival. Reprinted with permission.
Extract from http://www.cornwalls.co.uk © Cornwall Guide, 2014. Reprinted with permission.
Extract from http://www.westcornwallevents.co.uk © West Cornwall Events, 2014. Reprinted with permission.

Printed and bound in Thailand

2019 2018 2017 2016 2015
13 12 11 10 9 8 7 6 5